D0775368

DOES
SIZE
MATTER?

DOES
SIZE
MATTER?

APANDISIS
α
PUBLISHING

Apandisis Publishing
105 Madison Avenue, Suite 3A
New York, New York 10016

ISBN-13: 978-1-4127-5271-8
ISBN-10: 1-4127-5271-X

Manufactured in USA

8 7 6 5 4 3 2 1

www.FYIanswers.com

Contents

Chapter Two
LOVE AND LUST

Chapter Three
ORIGINS AND TRADITIONS

Chapter Four
BODY SCIENCE

Chapter Five
FOOD AND DRINK

Chapter Six
SPORTS

Chapter Seven
WEIRD SCIENCE AND TECHNOLOGY

Chapter Eight
HISTORY

Chapter Nine
HEALTH MATTERS

Chapter Ten
EARTH AND SPACE

Chapter Eleven
MORE GOOD STUFF

Introduction

D o you want to be the most interesting person in the world? Know stuff so fascinating and unusual that people eagerly gravitate toward you at parties in anticipation of your next story? Earn widespread adulation for your vast knowledge of weird and provocative topics? Win bar bets? Be a smart-ass about everything?

If you answered "yes" five times, you've come to the right book. *Does Size Matter?* provides answers to questions that most of us never even thought to ask. When cannibals are roasting poor, unfortunate Uncle Ed on a spit, have you ever wondered which part of him they are likely to fight over at mealtime? What is the tastiest part of the human body for cannibals? There is a real answer to this question, and you will find it in these pages, along with answers to many other questions that stretch the bounds of curiosity.

Does Size Matter? is a smart and authoritative narrative on myriad topics, ranging from body science to weird science, the animal kingdom to earth and space, love and lust to origins and traditions, and people to sports. Our writers demystify urban legends and inform on everything from the strange to the sublime.

Read *Does Size Matter?* and its companion book, *How Do Men Think?*, and you likely will come up with your own pressing questions for us to tackle. Go to our Web site, FYIanswers.com, to submit questions for future books and learn more about the F.Y.I. series. In the meantime, page through this offering and get smart.

Chapter One

ANIMAL KINGDOM

Q **If humans evolved from monkeys and apes, why are there still monkeys and apes?**

A Because humans didn't evolve from monkeys and apes. It's generally accepted in scientific circles that humans, monkeys, and apes all evolved from the same common ancestor. So somewhere in our past, we had an extremely apelike ancestor. Well, that's what they would look like to us. To apes, they'd look like an extremely humanlike ancestor. So why didn't that common ancestor evolve into just humans or apes? Why do we have both?

It boils down to our environments. Basically, the apelike ancestors who hung about in trees evolved to be really good at that.

Let's call them Climbers. Other apelike ancestors came down and ventured out onto the plains and became really good at that. They can be Walkers, since we're handing out names.

Wait! Quick recap of evolution: Many animals are born with small, random mutations. Mostly, these do nothing or result in death. But occasionally there's a really useful mutation, so that creature is better at, say, climbing trees than all of its friends. So it survives and has kids, who have the same mutations, and so on.

Right, carry on. So there were tree-dwelling Climbers and plains-dwelling Walkers. Eventually they evolved so far away from each other that they could no longer interbreed, and at this point they became two separate species. You can almost imagine them sadly waving goodbye to each other.

Debate about when humans actually split from other gorillalike apes rages on. Until fairly recently, it was believed that it happened somewhere between five and seven million years ago. But fossils found in Ethiopia in 2007 suggest that the split was more than ten million years ago. Science is like that. In any case, we first split from monkeys, because we share the fewest number of identical genes with them. Then we said goodbye to gibbons and orangutans, and finally we bid farewell to gorillas and chimpanzees. We share 98.4 percent of our DNA with chimps.

But why didn't all of those cute ape creatures die off, leaving only one direct descendant of the apelike ancestor? Haven't you been paying attention? They all filled out different evolutionary niches. Modern apes and monkeys are just as evolved as humans—they've just evolved in different ways. Watch them fling crud at each other and you'll realize we're not so different, really.

Q Do animals have recreational sex?

A Ah, the life of a dog owner. There's nothing like coming home from a hard day's work to find your faithful friend at the front door, wagging its tail in anticipation of your return. Fido bounds toward you, barking happily, and then...starts humping your leg. There aren't many dog owners who haven't had this dismaying experience. Why do dogs do this? Is your leg really that attractive?

For years, animal sexual behavior—such as Fido mounting your calf—often has been chalked up to instinct, the primal urge to pass on genetic material. It was Charles Darwin who postulated that procreation was a prime motive of animal sexuality. Animals mated only when the female was ovulating, this theory held, and she gave off very specific signs to the male when she was ready.

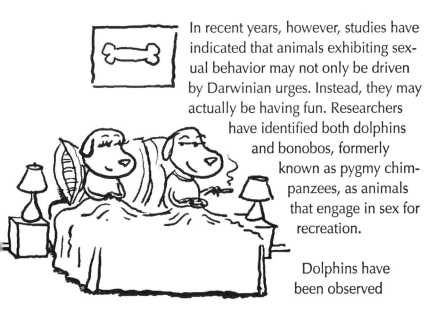

In recent years, however, studies have indicated that animals exhibiting sexual behavior may not only be driven by Darwinian urges. Instead, they may actually be having fun. Researchers have identified both dolphins and bonobos, formerly known as pygmy chimpanzees, as animals that engage in sex for recreation.

Dolphins have been observed

mating with each other even when the female is not ovulating. Bonobos take their sexual behavior one step further. Animal experts have witnessed bonobos masturbating, kissing with open mouths, engaging in homosexual behavior, and even participating in "makeup sex." However, researchers have yet to determine if bonobos have learned how to put on a Barry White album to get in the mood.

As for dogs, your leg is probably safe. Of course, if you come home one evening and find the foyer littered with rose petals, the two of you should probably have a talk.

Q How fast is a snail's pace?

A The word slow hardly begins to cover it. These animals make all others look like Speedy Gonzales. Next to the snail, tortoises look like hares, and hares look like bolts of furry brown lightning.

Which brings a bad joke to mind: What did the snail riding on the tortoise's back say?

Whee!

Garden snails have a top speed of about 0.03 mile per hour, according to *The World Almanac and Book of Facts*. However, snails observed in a championship race in London took the thirteen-inch course at a much slower rate—presumably because snails lack ambition when it comes to competition. To really get a snail moving, one would have to make the snail think its life was in jeopardy. Maybe the racing snails' owners should be hovering behind the starting line wearing feathered wings and pointed beaks, cawing instead of cheering.

The current record holder of the London race, the Guinness Gastropod Championship, is a snail named Archie, who made the trek in 1995 in two minutes and twenty seconds. This calculates to 0.0053 mile per hour. At that rate, a snail might cover a yard in 6.4 minutes. If he kept going, he might make a mile in a little less than eight days.

In the time it takes you to watch a movie, your pet snail might travel about fifty-six feet. You could watch a complete trilogy, and your snail might not even make it out of the house. Put your pet snail on the ground and forget about him—he'll be right around where you left him when you get back.

So long as no one steps on him, that is.

Q How much wood can a woodchuck chuck?

A "How much wood could a woodchuck chuck, if a woodchuck could chuck wood?"

This classic tongue twister has been part of the English lexicon for ages. But has anybody really thought about what it means? Has anybody even seen a woodchuck chucking wood? Or chucking anything, for that matter?

Part of the confusion lies in the origin of the word woodchuck. A woodchuck (*Marmota monax*) is, in fact, the same thing as a groundhog. In the Appalachians, it's known as a whistle pig. According to etymologists, the word woodchuck is probably derived from early colonial British settlers who bastardized *wuchak*, the local Native American word for groundhog. Because many early Americans couldn't be bothered to learn languages other than English (sort of like present-day Americans), they simply transformed the Algonquian word into one that sounded like English. That the name made absolutely no sense mattered little to these settlers, who were far more concerned with issues like starvation and massive epidemics of fatal illnesses.

Still, the question remains. What if woodchucks could chuck wood? Not surprisingly, there is little research on the topic. Indeed, no studies as of yet have proved that woodchucks are even capable of chucking wood, though there is ample evidence that woodchucks enjoy gnawing through wood when they encounter it.

There is, however, one thing that woodchucks are adept at chucking: dirt. The average woodchuck is quite a burrower, building complicated underground bunkers that would have made Saddam Hussein envious. These tunnels have been known to reach more than forty-five feet in length with a depth of several feet. Based on these measurements, one woodchuck expert determined that if the displaced dirt in a typical burrow was replaced with wood, the average whistle pig might be able chuck about seven hundred pounds of it.

In the end, the best answer is probably provided by the rhyme itself. "How much wood could a woodchuck chuck, if a woodchuck could chuck wood? A woodchuck would chuck all the wood he could, if a woodchuck could chuck wood." Which would probably be none.

Q Why do snakes shed their skin?

A All kinds of animals shed their skin, not only snakes. It's just that most species have the decency to do it in a less off-putting manner. Take humans. We shed about 1.5 million skin cells every hour, creating a new skin surface every twenty-eight days or so. But you don't see us walking around with huge pieces of dead skin hanging from our limbs—thank goodness for Vaseline Intensive Care.

The human skin-shedding process is ongoing, gradual, and relatively unnoticeable, while snakes shed quickly and completely, often in one long piece. Why do they do it that way? Sometimes it's to heal from an injury or remove parasites, but most of the time it's to accommodate growth. Most snakes shed at least four times over the course of a year. During the first few years of life, young snakes grow pretty rapidly, so they shed more frequently. Before a snake sheds, it tends to lay low for a week or two. During this period of inactivity, its eyes turn a cloudy, bluish-white color, and its vision is impaired. This tends to make a snake a bit nervous and unpredictable, so beware of any snake giving you a dull, blank stare.

After seven to fifteen days, the snake's eyes return to normal, and the skin shedding begins. The first skin to be dislodged is around the head, mouth, and nose (known as the rostrum). After that, the snake starts slinking around and between rough objects like branches and rocks to help it glide out of the old skin. This can take from a few hours to a few days, depending on environmental conditions and the health of the snake

The discarded skin of a snake can look like a dry, transparent tube or a moist, crumpled heap. Take a close-up peek at the head portion, and you'll see that a snake sheds everything—even its eye caps. One thing to note if you ever come across a snake's old skin: They often defecate at the same time they shed, so unless you're wearing gloves, it's wise to just look and not touch.

Q How do animals know when an earthquake is coming?

A One of the holy grails of scientific research is the ability to accurately predict earthquakes. The number of lives saved could be in the thousands per quake. It seems bizarre to think that animals are capable of something science has failed to accomplish, but evidence going back thousands of years suggests that animals know when an earthquake is coming. How do they do it?

We really have no idea. In fact, there is a great deal of debate as to whether animals actually have the ability to predict earthquakes, and few Western scientists consider the topic serious enough to research. Most of the evidence is anecdotal. No one has been able to duplicate predictive ability in a laboratory test, nor have any studies revealed what mechanism might allow for such predictive powers. The U.S. Geological Survey's official position on the matter is that "consistent and reliable behavior prior to seismic events, and a mechanism explaining how it could work, still eludes us."

There are many stories of animals acting strangely in the weeks, days, or hours preceding a quake. Examples include stampeding horses in Chile in 1835, snakes ending their hibernation early and leaving their holes in China in 1974, dogs and wolves howling incessantly in Italy in 1783, and the appearance of thousands of toads on a street in China in 2008. The stories involve a wide range of species and behaviors.

Skeptics suggest that the strange animal behavior is only linked to the earthquake event in hindsight, and that unusual behaviors occur all the time for any number of reasons (weather, hunger, the presence of other animals, etc.), but no one notices when an earthquake *doesn't* happen. Also, many of the reports come from places rather distant from the earthquake itself (the toads in China appeared three hundred and fifty miles away from the quake's epicenter), making the connection tenuous at best.

Chinese authorities have devoted a great deal of effort to earthquake prediction using animals, and they have claimed success in many cases. In 1975 they evacuated the city of Haicheng, and a few days later a large earthquake struck. Although Chinese officials reported that animal behavior was used for the prediction, it was later revealed that a series of foreshocks (rare pre-quake tremors) had been the real clue.

Suppose that animals *can* predict earthquakes—what physiological mechanism would be at work? One theory suggests that the movement of rocks deep below the surface of the earth releases electric energy that affects the earth's magnetic field and can be detected by animals. Others think the presence of magnetite, a magnetic mineral found in some animals, is the answer. Some species rely on the planet's magnetic field to orient their migration patterns, so a random pattern of magnetic fluctuations released by subsurface changes could drive the animals absolutely haywire.

Ultimately, it may be true that animals sense earthquakes in some way, but this ability is probably not reliable or accurate enough to allow humans to make any serious, useful earthquake predictions.

Q What is a pissant?

A You think a pissant is that smug, ninety-eight-pound-weakling of an usher who kicked you out of the box seats, even though the ballpark was half-empty. And technically, you're right. But call on an etymologist (or an entomologist), and you learn that aside from its occasional utility as the perfect insult, the word "pissant" does actually refer to a specific type of ant.

Some ants, among them the wood ant of northern Europe, produce pungent formic acid as a type of venom, which causes their mounds to smell like urine. This apparently had a profound effect on the noses of early speakers of the English language, because the word "pismire," an archaic term that means "an ant," stems from the Middle English word "pissemyre." "Pisse" means exactly what you would think it means—okay, "piss" or "urine" for those who don't have enough of an imagination to figure it out—and "myre" appears to be Scandinavian in origin, akin to the Danish word *myre*, which means ant.

Over the years, we've dropped the formality and gone straight for the more blunt "pissant." And you have to admit, that's just a lot more fun to hiss at an usher, or any other insignificant member of our species.

Q Can plants eat animals?

A We tend to think of plants as passive organisms. They're immobile, rooted into the ground, and if they move at all it's to placidly, slowly grow in the direction of the sun. They survive on sunlight and water. Yet there are plants that supplement their diets by absorbing nutrients from the digested bodies of dead insects. They are carnivorous plants.

The best-known carnivorous plant is the Venus flytrap. A rare and unique plant, the Venus flytrap has a freaky method of snapping shut to enclose and kill a wayward insect. When an insect touches the trigger hairs within the curved leaves that form the plant's trap, the leaves spring shut through a mechanism that scientists do not fully understand. According to a Harvard professor of applied math and mechanics, a change in the water pressure of the leaves causes them to alter their shape from convex to concave. Once the plant has trapped its prey, it secretes enzymes that dissolve the unfortunate bug into a nutritious liquid that the plant can absorb directly. Everything but the exoskeleton is digested.

Why did plants ever evolve such a bizarre way of getting nutrients? Most carnivorous plant species are native to areas with poor soil. Nitrogen from the soil is just as important to plants as sun and water. Unable to get enough through their roots, these plants evolved a means to absorb nitrogen from the decomposing bodies of insects.

The Venus flytrap is not the only carnivorous plant species. Many other plants "eat" animals through more passive means. Pitcher plants have leaves that form a shape like a tall cup lined with downward-pointing hairs that keep an insect from escaping once it is trapped inside. The insect drowns in the plant's "stomach," which brims with digestive acid enzymes. Sundews and rainbow plants secrete a sticky mucus on their leaves, creating their own version of flypaper. The mucus not only attracts and traps insects, but also suffocates and dissolves them. There's also the bladderwort, which has a doorlike mechanism that, when signaled by its trigger hairs, opens to allow its prey in but won't let it out.

If all this talk of carnivorous plants has you feeling a little concerned about your next walk through the woods, relax. None of the species gets large or strong enough to eat even the smallest mammals.

Q How long can a camel go without water?

A No, they aren't adorable like puppies, kittens, or panda bears. Camels have three eyelids, big lumpy humps on their backs, and are just plain weird-looking. But in the desert, a camel would leave a trail of puppy, kitten, and panda bodies behind—all of them dead from dehydration. So the camel has that going for it.

Camels have a special place to keep water, and it isn't in their humps. Both the Dromedary (one-hump) camel and the Bactrian (two-hump) camel have oval-shaped red blood cells; all other mammals have circular ones. These special oval-shaped red blood cells make blood flow easier when the animal is in a dehydrated state. Additionally, the oval shape allows a camel to drink amazing quantities of water—more than twenty gallons!—in one sitting. Though this much water would send most mammals into shock, a camel's red blood cells can expand to hold the water without rupturing.

Camels also take full advantage of the water in the food they eat. Depending on the plant, they can efficiently use the water contained within, which buys them time before they need a drink. Their kidneys are the king of kidneys, pulling every nutrient and useful bit from ingested water before turning the leftovers into extremely thick and salty urine.

Additionally, a camel can tolerate extreme fluctuations in body temperature. Humans have a fever when their temperature rises only one or two degrees above the norm. But a camel is perfectly fine with a body temperature anywhere between 93 and 106 degrees Fahrenheit. This means that a camel can get pretty hot without needing to sweat to cool itself—a characteristic that allows the beast to keep all that precious water inside its body.

The combination of the camel's unique red blood cells, its ability to "take the heat," and its highly efficient kidney and intestinal system enables it to go a week or more without needing water. The actual length of time depends on how hard the camel is working (it can handle hundreds of pounds of weight), how hot the climate is, and how fast it has to move. While a person may live only two or three days without water while riding around on a camel in hundred-degree heat, the camel could live for a week or more.

So here's to the camel—it won't be winning any beauty contests, but it is definitely a front-runner in nature's talent competition.

Q Can chickens really run around after their heads are cut off?

A You bet they can! If you thought this was just an expression for being in a frenzied state, think again.

When a chicken is decapitated, its brain is severed from its spine, and any voluntary control over movement ceases. However, a chicken's involuntary movements—say, running around like it just lost its head—are controlled by electrical impulses, which originate at the spinal cord and continue until the muscles themselves run out of energy. As for the length of time a chicken can run around post-beheading, that depends on the chicken.

If your stomach isn't already turning, chew on this less-than-savory story about the famous Mike, a Wyandotte rooster that lived for a whopping eighteen months after its head was detached. On September 10, 1945, Mike's owner, farmer Lloyd Olsen of Fruita, Colorado, quite awkwardly tried to behead the five-and-a-half-month-old feathered fellow in preparation for a meal for his mother-in-law. Alas, Olsen missed the jugular vein (a blood clot prevented Mike from bleeding to death), and left one ear and most of the brain stem intact. That night, poor Mike slept with its severed head tucked beneath its wing.

Mike survived, and attempted to walk, hunt, peck, preen, and gurgle in place of crowing. A milk-and-water mixture and some grains were fed to the bird via an eyedropper, helping it grow to a strapping eight pounds. Olsen and his family molded a successful showbiz career for Mike, which included twenty-five-cent side-show appearances across the nation and photographs for popular magazines, such as *Time* and *Life*.

Mike earned up to $4,500 a month and was valued at $10,000. But don't cry fowl at these exploitations and indignities—it was the consensus of humane society groups that the rooster didn't suffer. Unfortunately (or fortunately), Mike met his demise in a Phoenix motel in March 1947, when the Olsens were unable to swiftly locate an eyedropper to clear mucus from Mike's throat.

Today, residents of Fruita pay their own wacky tribute to the fallen rooster with a Mike the Headless Chicken Web site (www.miketheheadlesschicken.org), complete with pictures of the headless hero strutting his stuff. They even celebrate Mike's unusual life with an annual festival held the third weekend in May. Considering all of this fuss, the question needs to be asked: Who exactly lost their heads?

Q Why do pigeons live in cities?

A They aren't historic landmarks, but the flocks of pigeons populating the parks and buildings of New York are as much a part of the city as Times Square or the Empire State Building. Pigeons are also abundant in Chicago, London, Paris, and other big cities around the world. Most of the time the news surrounding pigeons is about how much of a nuisance they are, so you might be wondering if they're hanging around your city just to wreak havoc.

There are hundreds of species of *Columbidae*, the bird family comprising both pigeons and doves (the words "pigeon" and "dove" can be used interchangeably, although the former is usually used for smaller birds and the latter for larger ones). They live in all sorts of habitats; Antarctica is the only continent without at least one species of pigeon.

The bird that most urban dwellers know as a pigeon is a descendant of the Rock Pigeon, the oldest domesticated bird species in the world. Pigeons have been raised for food, used as messengers during times of war, kept as pets, and trained to race. Those domesticated pigeons escaped captivity and continued to breed, giving rise to massive flocks of feral birds. In the wild, the Rock Pigeon prefers to nest and roost in rocky cliffs, so the rooftops and window ledges in large cities make a good substitute.

Pigeons also prosper in cities due to a side effect of all those people—the massive amounts of food left lying around. They never have to worry about finding their next meal; it's either coming from the kindly old gent on the bench or the trashcan full of fast-food wrappers next to him. Natural enemies of pigeons, such as owls, hawks, and raccoons, don't tend to live in cities. The abundance of food and good nesting sites combined with the absence of predators make cities the perfect habitat...from the point of view of the pigeon, anyway.

Pigeons are often called "rats with wings," and it's true that they can spread some diseases through their droppings. But they have also served important roles in history. If you happen to be in a city with lots of pigeons and one makes you its unfortunate victim, just remember that it might be a descendant of a decorated pigeon like G.I. Joe, which carried messages for the Allies during World War II.

Q What eats sharks?

A One of the most feared animals in the world, the shark has a reputation for being a people killer, ruthlessly nibbling on a leg or an arm just to see how it tastes. But in the shark vs. people debate, guess who loses? Yup, sharks. We eat way more of them than they do of us. And we aren't the only ones partaking in their sharkliciousness.

For the most part, the big predator sharks are in a pretty cushy position ecologically. As apex predators, they get to do the eating without all that pesky struggle to keep from being eaten. They are important to the ecosystem because they keep everything below them in check so there are no detrimental population booms. For example, sharks eat sea lions, which eat mollusks. If no one ate sea lions, they'd thrive and eat all the mollusks. So if sharks are apex predators (so are humans, by the way), they aren't ever eaten, right? Wrong. Sometimes a shark gets a hankering for an extra-special treat: another shark.

Tiger sharks start eating other sharks in the womb: Embryonic tiger sharks will eat their less-developed brothers and sisters. This tradition of eating fellow tiger sharks continues through adult-

hood. And great white sharks have been found with four- to seven-foot-long sharks in their stomachs, eaten whole.

There's also what is called a feeding frenzy. What generally happens is that an unusual prey (shipwreck survivors, for example) presents itself and attracts local sharks, which devour the unexpected meal. The sharks get so worked up from the frenzied feeding, they might turn on each other.

Orcas and crocodiles have also been known to snack on shark when the opportunity presents itself. Note that both orca and crocodiles are also apex predators. So while there are no sea-faring animals that live on shark and shark alone, sharks aren't totally safe.

Finally, there's that irksome group of animals known as humans. Many people who reside in Asia regularly partake of shark fin soup, among other dishes prepared with shark ingredients.

Through over-fishing, humans reduced the shortfin mako's population in the Atlantic Ocean by 68 percent between 1978 and 1994.

Even with all this crazy shark-eating, it's a good bet a sea lion or mackerel would happily trade places with the apex predator any day of the week.

Q Is spider silk really the strongest material in the world?

A No—but it comes remarkably close.

The strongest material in the world has been recognized as the carbon nanotube, which is fifty times stronger than steel. These are microscopic, tubelike molecules of carbon, smaller in diameter than a strand of hair.

Spider silk, on the other hand, is five times as strong as steel and is comparable in strength to Kevlar (the material used to make bullet-proof vests). Spider silk can stretch to 130 percent of its length before breaking and is estimated to withstand up to six hundred thousand pounds of pressure per square inch.

A composite material made up of crystalline molecules, spider silk puts synthetic materials to shame in terms of the range of applications for which it might be used. "Liquid crystal," as it's called by the science community, has achieved perfection after four hundred million years of evolution, and lately it's getting scientists' panties all in a bunch.

Spider silk has been studied with envy for some time now, and there have been various attempts at domesticating spiders with the intention of harvesting the material. None of these have panned out, mostly because spiders cannot stand to live in close quarters with other spiders. They need room to live, and they will kill any other spider that cramps their space. Because of this, spider farming was ruled out of the question early in the silk-production game.

But a Canadian company called Nexia Biotechnologies has lately stumbled upon an answer. Through bioengineering, the company's scientists have been able to produce mass quantities of orb spider silk in the mammary glands of goats. The scientists take cells from one goat, mix them with specific spider genes in a culture dish, and then transfer the cells into unfertilized eggs. (The process is similar to that which produced Dolly, the world's first cloned sheep.) The resulting male goats are then put out to stud. Females born from this breeding produce spider-silk proteins in their mammary glands. These proteins are extracted from the milk and mechanically spun into fiber.

There has been success in fostering a spider's silk proteins in other mammals—and in some plants, to a limited extent—but goats have been particularly adept at producing the proteins. The speed at which female goats mature, and the ease of caring for the animals, likely played a part in their selection for this particular task.

Nexia intends to put the material to a variety of uses, including fishing line, sutures, tennis racket strings, body armor, and even replacement tendons. Spider silk appears to be the perfect material for each of these tasks, based on strength, flexibility, and biodegradability.

It's not perfect yet—natural silk contains seven different proteins, while the silk produced in the goats' mammary glands contains just one—but Nexia's scientists are working on the problem. While they're at it, they might want to give some thought to the company's marketing plan. Spiderweb tennis rackets will be all the rage until the players get out on the court and find they can't even complete a single volley. Soon to follow will be a wave of rackets returned to the manufacturers with tennis balls stuck in the middle of the webbing.

Q What makes a firefly's butt glow?

A Fireflies are nature's night pilots, diving and swooping like tiny prop planes, communicating their location and intent with a series of flashing lights. To potential predators, these lights say, "Stay away." To potential mates, they say, "Come hither." To a child running around the yard with a Mason jar, they can mean a lamp that will grow brighter and more fascinating with each bug that is caught.

Like all animals possessing bioluminescent traits, fireflies produce their light by means of chemical reaction. The bugs manufacture a chemical known as luciferin. Through a reaction powered by adenosine triphosphate and an enzyme called luciferase, luciferin is transformed into oxyluciferin. In the firefly, this reaction takes place in the abdomen, an area perforated by tubes that allow oxygen to enter, feed the chemical reaction, and become bonded to the luciferin and luciferase produced by the insect. Oxyluciferin is a chemical that contains charged electrons; these electrons release their charge immediately, and the product of this release is light.

All fireflies emit light in the larvae stage. This is thought to be a warning sign to animals looking for snacks: Chemicals in the firefly's (and the firefly larvae's) body have a bitter taste that is undesirable to predators. Studies have shown that laboratory mice quickly learn to associate the bioluminescent glow with a bad taste, and they avoid food that radiates this light.

In adult fireflies, bioluminescence has a second purpose: Some species of firefly use their glow—and distinctive patterns made by dipping and swooping, in which they draw simple patterns against the black of night—to attract a mate. Each firefly species, of which there are 1,900 worldwide, has its own pattern. Male fireflies flit about and show off, while the females sit in a tree or in the grass. The females will not give off light until they see a male displaying the wattage and sprightliness they're looking for in an attractive mate.

They must choose carefully, however, as there are certain adult firefly species that are unable to manufacture luciferin on their own. These species obtain the chemical by attracting unwitting members of other species and consuming them. They do this because without the chemical, they appear to predators much as any other night-flying insects; they need the chemical to advertise their bitter taste.

In the end, this effort might be for naught. The flavor particular to the firefly has that special something that some frogs cannot get enough of. For these frogs, the blinking lights are not so much a warning as a sign reading, "Come and get it!"

Q Who decides which bee gets to be queen?

A Unlike the human business world, where grunts toil at their desks while the CEO zips in and out of his big corner office and hardly notices his minions, workers are the ones who hold the cards in a bee colony. In fact, they decide which bee gets to be queen.

A queen bee typically lives five to seven years. When she begins laying fewer eggs or becomes diseased, worker bees decide her reign has run its course. No golden parachute is provided, just a process called supersedure.

What's involved in supersedure? Workers quickly build a peanut-shaped queen cell, and a larva is raised in it. While this larva is identical to what develops into a worker bee, another average Joe isn't on the way. The larva for the queen is fed large amounts of a protein-rich secretion called royal jelly, which comes from glands on the heads of young workers.

After about two weeks, the new queen emerges. Just as two bosses are not good for business in the human world, the new queen seeks out the old queen and stings her to death. (Unlike the stinger of a proletariat bee, the queen's is not barbed and will not detach from her body upon contact with her victim. This means she can sting repeatedly without dying.) Reproduction is the key role for the queen because female worker bees are sterile. About a week after doing in her predecessor, the new queen takes her nuptial flights, mating high in the air with male drones. Then she begins her job of laying eggs.

Sometimes, though, things don't unfold as planned for the queen-to-be. Just as bosses in the human world don't like surrendering the big corner office, the established queen doesn't always go easily. There are occasions when the reigning queen defeats the aspiring one. When this happens, everything remains as it was in the hive—until another young challenger comes along and attempts to slay the queen.

The bees themselves don't always dictate the fate of a bee colony. Beekeepers, whose job it is to harvest honey, can initiate supersedure in the colonies they maintain. When beekeepers notice that the queen is laying fewer eggs, they clip off one of her middle or posterior legs, which prevents her from properly placing her eggs at the bottom of the cell. Workers detect this deficiency, and the queen is eventually killed off.

And you thought corporate America was cutthroat.

Q Would cockroaches really survive a nuclear war?

A We've all heard that cockroaches would be the only creatures to survive a nuclear war. But unless being exceptionally gross is a prerequisite for withstanding such an event, are cockroaches really that resilient?

They are indeed. For one thing, they've spent millions of years surviving every calamity the earth could throw at them. Fossil records indicate that the cockroach is at least three hundred million years old. That means cockroaches survived unscathed whatever event wiped out the dinosaurs, be it an ice age or a giant meteor's collision with Earth.

The cockroach's chief advantage—at least where nuclear an-
nihilation is concerned—is the amount of radiation it can safely
absorb. During the Cold War, a number of researchers performed
tests on how much radiation various organisms could withstand
before dying. Humans, as you might imagine, tapped out fairly
early. Five hundred Radiation Absorbed Doses (or rads, the
accepted measurement for radiation exposure) are fatal to
humans. Cockroaches, on the other hand, scored exceptionally
well, withstanding up to 6,400 rads.

Such hardiness doesn't mean that cockroaches will be the sole
rulers of the planet if nuclear war breaks out. The parasitoid wasp
can take more than 100,000 rads and still sting the hell out of
you. Some forms of bacteria can shrug off more than one million
rads and keep doing whatever it is that bacteria do. Clearly, the
cockroach would have neighbors.

Not all cockroaches would survive, anyway—definitely not
the ones that lived within two miles of the blast's ground zero.
Regardless of the amount of radiation a creature could withstand, the intense heat from the detonation would liquefy it. Still,
the entire cockroach race wouldn't be living at or near ground
zero—so, yes, at least some would likely survive. But they'd still
be cockroaches. And how much fun would that be?

Q Why do a cat's eyes shine in the dark?

A Ever see a cat's eyes shining at night? Pretty weird, right?
How do cats do that? Do they use their eyes like we use

headlights on a car—to find their way in the dark? To a certain degree, they do.

Cats have a special layer of cells in their eyes known as the *tapetum lucidum* (Latin for "shining carpet"). The *tapetum* is located behind the retina and acts as a mirror, catching and reflecting light. A cat's retina is composed of rods and cones, just like a human retina.

Cones are responsible for daylight vision and the ability to see colors; rods are used in night vision and for detecting sudden movements. As you may guess, night hunters, including cats, have eyes with a high ratio of rods to cones—twenty-five to one. (Human eyes have only four rods to every cone, which is why we have poor night vision.)

The *tapetum lucidum* is essentially a back-up system for the rods in the cat's retina. The tightly clustered rods catch most of the available light at night, but some light inevitably slips by the rods. When this happens in humans, the light is simply absorbed by the back of the retina and lost—we can't use it to see. But in cats' eyes, this lost light hits the *tapetum* and is reflected back through the retina via the rods, giving these sensitive cells a second chance to use the light to enhance the cat's vision. This reflective process is what creates those spooky headlight eyes that have inspired so many Halloween cards.

In addition to the *tapetum*, the cat's elliptically shaped pupils give it an advantage at night. Cats' pupils can dilate very rapidly to fill almost the entire iris, letting in even more light. Some scientists think that the elliptical shape of the pupil enables the eye to utilize a wider–than–normal range of light waves, further enhancing vision. But this is only a theory—it's not a proven fact.

Other animals—including dogs, deer, fruit bats, dolphins, and some species of fish—have the *tapetum lucidum*, too, though its effects are not as pronounced as in cats. Research on the *tapetum lucidum* has been useful to the field of thin film optics, and has been applied to the development of mirrors and reflective lights to aid human night vision.

We will probably never be able to equal the cat's ability to see in the dark, however. Feline eyes are a unique and beautiful evolutionary adaptation. And a bit of Halloween, 365 nights a year.

Q Why do bats sleep upside down?

A Bats sure are show-offs. Not only are they the sole mammals that can fly without going through airport security, not only can they snag hundreds of bugs an hour using built-in sonar, but they also like to catch their Zzzzs while dangling from a rocky cave ceiling. Meanwhile, the rest of us have trouble dozing off without our special pillow, fluffy blankie, and night-night snack.

The first logical question is, why do bats sleep this way in the first place (other than to impress chicks)? Because while bats are hotshots in the air, they're pretty sorry walkers. With only tiny, girlyman legs to prop them up, there's no way bats can get the running start they need to take off. Instead, they just drop from a high spot and start flying.

So it's a lot safer for them to sleep in the takeoff position, in case they need to hightail it at a moment's notice. As an added bonus, sleeping this way keeps them out of reach of curious toddlers and other vicious predators.

But how do they do it? If you were to try to hang upside down in a cave, you would flex muscles in your feet, which would pull on tendons connected to your toes, making your toes clench around the rock.

Bats take out the middleman. Tendons run from the bat's claws directly to the bat's body. The bat grabs onto the rock and just relaxes. Its body weight pulls down on the tendons, locking the claws shut. Bats actually have to flex their muscles to unclench the rock.

In fact, if a bat kicks the bucket in its sleep, it will just hang there as the body decomposes. Even in death, these creatures can't help showboating.

Chapter Two

LOVE AND LUST

Q Does size matter?

A   The United States is a nation that enjoys big things. We buy McMansions with more rooms than we can use at prices we can't afford. We eat at restaurants whose portion sizes are suitable for a race of Brobdingnagians. We somehow believe that we need to drink fountain beverages out of containers the size of the Stanley Cup. And in locker rooms all across the country, men with average-size penises, envious of the guys in the shower stall next to them, decide to trade in their SUVs for even larger vehicles.

From fast food to real estate to anatomy, the American public has delivered its verdict: Size does matter. And in almost all cases, we do, indeed, seem to think that bigger is better.

Perhaps nowhere does the obsession over size manifest itself more than in our concern about sexual anatomy. The rate of women undergoing breast augmentation surgery has skyrocketed by nearly 500 percent in the past decade, while desperate men are spending millions of dollars each year on useless supplements purporting to increase penis size. Yet few pause in their frenzied quest for girth, length, and cup size to wonder exactly to whom their size matters.

In reality, it only seems to matter to themselves. One survey found that while nearly 55 percent of men wish they were better endowed, only 15 percent of women are dissatisfied with their partner's penis size—and, in fact, are far more interested in the shape of the penis than its size. On the flip side, survey after survey indicates that men decidedly prefer smaller natural breasts over large fake ones. Yet a recent study found that women who undergo breast enhancement surgery experience concomitantly inflated levels of self-esteem, even though, ironically, more men might find them less attractive.

So why, in the face of crushing evidence that bigger is not better, do we still worship at the altar of enormity? If sociobiologists are correct, our bizarre desire for all things large comes down to—you guessed it—sex.

Some sociobiologists root our desire for all things large to a primitive biological urge to pass on our genetic material. These sociobiologists argue that way back in the caveman days, large, well-shaped penises indicated to the female that the male was more likely to reproduce. Meanwhile, large, well-shaped breasts indicated to the male that the female was fertile and more apt to have his child.

Other scientists disagree. One theory points out that the average penis size of a human male is far larger than is needed to deliver sperm. According to this theory, larger penis sizes developed as a result of male-to-male competition, which had ramifications for social order and power. This evolutionary game of "mine is bigger than yours" is still with us to this day, translating to gas-guzzling vehicles, soulless suburban mansions, and Super Big Gulps that hold enough Mr. Pibb to caffeinate the population of Vermont.

Ironically, the primal urge toward largeness may not be well placed. While evolutionary models do seem to reward larger members of a given species, they also indicate that bigger species go extinct more quickly. If only the same could be said for certain unwieldy consumer products.

Q Can a person masturbate too much?

A Hairy palms. Blindness. Insanity. People have been told for ages that they will contract some terrible affliction if they masturbate. Considering the relatively large number of sane people walking around with perfect sight and smooth hands, it seems unlikely that these old wives' tales hold much truth. (Not that we don't still check our palms for peach fuzz every now and then.) But even if you won't go blind, is it possible to masturbate too much?

According to masturbation theorists (yes, they really *do* exist), for much of history, masturbation wasn't the taboo subject that it is today. Of course, most religions denounced it as wasteful and sinful. But for the ancient Greeks, masturbation was only evil in the sense that *all* sexual desire was evil. To Socrates and his cronies, sexual expression was morally inferior to sexual abstinence, including abstinence from masturbating. (Of course, that didn't stop Socrates from playing with teenage boys.)

But by and large, masturbation was commonplace: Ancient paintings and tapestries depicted the act. Plays, stories, and jokes incorporated masturbation into their punch lines. In fact, seventeenth-century diarist Samuel Pepys once bragged that he was able to bring himself to completion by merely imagining a girl he'd seen earlier in the day; he also crowed that the sight of the Queen and her ladies in church so excited him that he had to masturbate right then and there.

By the mid-nineteenth century, however, as social mores became increasingly restrictive, the idea of a connection between masturbation and disease was cemented; this idea culminated in the laughable prudery of the Victorian era. In a society where even piano legs were covered with trousers, masturbation was unspeakable. During this time, historians say, masturbating came to be associated with such maladies as blindness, hairy palms, deafness, mental retardation, and insanity.

With the rise of Freudian thought and the release of the Kinsey Reports in the twentieth century, sex became a far less taboo subject. Nowadays, masturbation is still ripe material for comedy—just ask the Farrelly brothers. Sex experts agree that masturbation is healthy and normal, and estimate that more than 90 percent of men and 60 percent of women jack and jill. Furthermore, the only physical ailments you're likely to suffer from these sessions are cramped fingers and raw, chafed genitals.

Masturbation can be problematic, however, when it becomes more important than interacting with the world. For some, excessive masturbation is an escape from emotional or relational issues that would be better remedied through discussion or therapy. But for most people, too much masturbation isn't a concern.

Masturbation has even found wider social acceptance. Bands, including Green Day, openly reference the deed; groups, such as the San Francisco Jacks, are dedicated to the celebration and practice of it. Academia, too, has embraced it: Increasing numbers of academics research the field of "masturbation theory." Sort of gives the term "ivory tower" a new meaning, doesn't it?

Q Do prostitutes file tax returns?

A If you feel like you get screwed by the IRS every year at tax time, quit complaining—how do you think prostitutes feel? At least you're only getting screwed once.

In one of the great ironies of the American social system, prostitutes—who can go to prison in nearly every state for plying their trade—can also get jail time for not paying taxes on that ill-gotten lucre. According to the IRS, all self-employment income in excess of four hundred dollars must be reported and taxed, regardless of the source. This is how gangster Al Capone was famously put away: tax evasion (though his income didn't come through prostitution).

In Nevada, where prostitution is legal, prostitutes are classified as "independent contractors," receive 1099-MISC forms, and are expected to pay self-employment taxes. Many prostitutes, regardless of their legality, want to be good citizens, and do pay income tax. Indeed, there is even an organization in New York that's dedicated to assisting sex workers in filing their income taxes.

Bad things can happen to prostitutes who fail to pay their taxes. In 2006, the Senate Judiciary Committee passed a bill establishing a unit that is responsible for investigating pimps and prostitutes who evade tax laws. Given some of the tawdry links between government officials and sex workers in recent years, there's no telling what such investigations could expose.

Q Does a man have a G-spot?

A Technically speaking, men don't have G-spots. The G-spot is named after Ernst Grafenberg, a German gynecologist and sex researcher; the term also refers to the paraurethral glands, which are located within the front wall of the vagina. The male counterpart to this is the prostate—more specifically, the prostate and the perineum.

The prostate is a walnut-size gland that surrounds the upper section of the urethra (the tube inside the penis, through which urine and semen pass). When a man's penis is erect, the prostate becomes swollen and closes off the urethra.

The perineum, unlike the prostate, is located on the outside of the body. It's a dime-size, spongy spot between the anus and scrotum.

The key nerves controlling erection, orgasm, and ejaculation come together at the prostate and the perineum. Simply put, these regions are the headquarters for male sexual pleasure. The *Kama Sutra,* Tantric sex guides, and Taoist beliefs all recommend prostate massage to expand a man's capacity for sexual power, pleasure, and overwhelming ecstasy; as a side benefit, prostate massage has been viewed as a way to maintain and increase sexual health for men since ancient times.

About a hundred years ago, when your great-grandparents thought they were trendsetters, many women used a steel apparatus to manually massage their men's prostates during lovemaking. Such items were so commonplace and widely used that they were sold at the local five-and-dime or at the drugstore.

During World War II, Armed Forces medics gave prostate massages to soldiers who hadn't had sex for some time, usually after sixty to ninety days. These massages were said to be a method of managing pelvic congestion. No word on whether the wives back home considered it cheating.

Q Is it okay to marry your cousin?

A It sure is, at least in some parts of the world. Take Saudi Arabia. According to the *New York Times*, the Saudi government reports that 55 to 70 percent of marriages are between blood relatives. In fact, across the Arab world, 45 percent of all married couples are related, according to Dr. Nadia Sakati, a senior consultant for the genetics research center at King Faisal Specialist Hospital in Riyadh, Saudi Arabia.

In Pakistan (where cousin marriage is traditional and arranged) and Indonesia, the thought is that when you marry a family member, you know with whom you are dealing. It also preserves parental control and ensures that any wealth will stay in the family, although this is considered less important.

In China, there are some sixty million girls who would have been viable candidates for marriage if not for gender-based abortions and female infanticide, so a man sometimes has little choice but to marry a close family member (though not if it's his paternal uncle's daughter, as patrilateral parallel cousin marriage is forbidden). In the United States, marrying one's cousin brings up subjects such as incest and inbreeding, and conjures up images of a banjo-playing boy and homosexual hillbillies from the 1970s cult film *Deliverance*.

The taboo attached to consanguineous marriage (cousin marrying) in the United States dates back to the nineteenth century, when westbound settlers wanted to distinguish themselves from Native Americans. Among other things, they proposed that no "white man" marry his cousin, because that is what the "savages" did.

However, anthropologists say that male Native Americans had no need to marry their female kin because there were plenty of other women available. Male European settlers, on the other hand, had fewer non-kin women from which to choose from, and some did marry within their bloodlines.

Not only is marrying your cousin taboo in the United States, it is illegal in some areas. Twenty-four states have laws that make it a crime to marry your first cousin, and five other states permit the union only if the couple is incapable of reproducing. These laws, in most cases, have been on the books for more than a century and are considered outdated, especially when the latest findings on the subject of consanguineous marriages are taken into consideration.

The National Society of Genetic Counselors (NSGC), a leading authority in the field, funded a study that found that children born to first-cousin couples are at only slightly higher risk for genetic disorders such as cystic fibrosis, Tay Sachs, or congenital

heart defects. The offspring of a "normal" couple have a 3 to 4 percent chance of having these defects, and children of a first-cousin couple have an increased risk of only 1.7 to 2.8 percent.

The offspring of second cousins who marry are in the normal range for birth defects. Based on the NSGC's findings, which involved the review of six major studies conducted from 1965 to 2000 that involved several thousand births, the organization concluded that there is no biological reason for first cousins not to marry.

This would be a relief to some famous persons who married their first cousins: Queen Victoria, Edgar Allan Poe, Charles Darwin, Jesse James, and H. G. Wells. Not enough star power for you in that group? Okay, then you might want to consult the 1913 *Catholic Encyclopedia*, which contains an entry speculating that Mary and Joseph, the mother and father of Jesus, were first cousins.

Q Is sex fun at age eighty?

A Back in the day, people wanted merely to live to see the ripe old age of eighty. Now, scientific advancements have not only lengthened the time one can spend on the planet, but also have improved a person's ability to have sex at an advanced age. Men in their eighties, nineties, and beyond are waking up with morning wood, right up until they are ready to be put into a pine box. Sure, it is an erection induced by Viagra, Cialis, or Levitra—but who is complaining?

Women never lose their ability to have sex; in the past, a lack of willing and able partners was the problem. Today, condoms are passed out at assisted living facilities because senior citizens are the latest faces on the STD block. Octogenarian women are getting their freak on with ancient men who up until 1998—when Viagra came on the market—were more concerned with a hip break than a hip thrust.

Now that you know your grandparents might still be having sex, you need to find out if they are having fun. The sheer quantity of erectile dysfunction medications, lubricants, and condoms that are sold to the elderly—and the number of sex seminars presented at retirement homes—should be evidence enough that sex is fun at age eighty. Here's a prime example: The king of all sex-having octogenarians, Hugh Hefner, claimed in an interview in the September 2007 issue of *Details* magazine that he has three—count 'em, three—live-in lovers, and that he has sex several times a week. Here's an excerpt:

How important is sex to you now that you are in your eighties, Mr. Hefner?

"I still have sex several times a week. But when you talk about sex, it's the intimacy that matters."

There's a belief that the afterlife is somehow better than the life we have now.

"Not better than my life! Jay Leno once said, 'If there is a heaven, where's Hefner going to go?'"

Q What are the ingredients of Love Potion No. 9?

A We thought we should ask, just in case you're looking to hook up with that cute barista at the corner coffee shop. Love potions have long been credited with having major magical influences over the whims and woes of human attraction. And they just might work.

In the second century AD, Roman writer and philosopher Apuleius allegedly concocted a potion that snagged him a rather wealthy widow. Relatives of the widow even brought Apuleius to court, claiming the witchy potion had worked to subvert the woman's true wishes. Apuleius argued that the potion (supposedly made with shellfish, lobsters, spiced oysters, and cuttlefish) had restored his wife's vivacity and spirit—and the court ended up ruling in his favor.

Yes, love potions have been the stuff of history and mystical legend since ancient times. These alluring elixirs played a major role in Greek and Egyptian mythology, and even made an appearance in the 2004 fairy-tale flick *Shrek 2*. In the movie, the Fairy Godmother gives the King of Far Far Away a bottled potion intended to make Fiona fall in love with the first man she kisses.

That bottle was marked with a Roman numeral IX, by the way, a clear nod to the formula first made famous in the doo-wop ditty "Love Potion No. 9," which was recorded by The Clovers in 1959 and The Searchers in 1963. According to the song, as penned by legendary songwriters Jerry Leiber and Mike Stoller, the ingredients for the concoction "smelled like turpentine, and looked like Indian ink."

Doesn't sound too appealing, huh? Well, it apparently did enough to help a guy who was "a flop with chicks." That is, until he "kissed a cop down on 34th and Vine."

At any rate, if you're a forlorn lover looking to make a little magic of your own, you just might be in luck. In the mid-1990s, Leiber and Stoller worked with former guitarist and part-time perfumer Mara Fox to develop a trademarked cologne spray bearing the name of their hit song.

According the label, Love Potion #9 is made with water, SD40B alcohol, isopropyl myristate, isopropyl alcohol, and the fragrances of citrus and musk. Can this cool, clean scent really heighten your passion and arousal and make you attractive to the opposite sex?

Hey, if George Clooney or Angelina Jolie happens to be in the area, it's certainly worth a spritz! However, the perfume does come with a disclaimer: "No guarantee of success is granted or implied."

Q Why are wedding dresses white?

A Billy Idol once sang about it being a nice day for a white wedding, and just about any groom would agree. White is symbolic of the bride's purity, which means the groom can imagine that he's the first man to ever lay hands on her.

Obviously, this is more fairy tale than reality. Times have changed, and the tradition of a woman wearing white on her wedding day has been distilled down to a style option rather than a symbol of her virginity. But a guy can dream, can't he?

Queen Victoria, who married Albert of Saxe-Coburg in 1840, is most frequently credited with starting the trend of wearing a white wedding dress. However, in 1499 Anne of Brittany married Louis XII in a white dress, and Mary Queen of Scots married François II of France in 1558 while clad in white. This was a most boorish fashion statement on Mary's part since, at that time, white was the official color of mourning in France. It goes to show how she felt about the arranged nuptials.

Prior to these royals being wed in white, most brides were married in bright colors, which signified their joy. Any color was suitable. Well, almost any. Black was not considered appropriate, because that was the color for mourning; red, meanwhile, was reserved for prostitutes, at least in Western cultures. (In some Asian countries, red, the color of good luck, was and continues to be a traditional hue for a wedding dress.) Green also was frowned upon in Western cultures, partially because it is the color of foliage and some thought it might encourage rain.

Bright colors turned to white, however, after Queen Victoria strode down the aisle. In 1849 *Godey's Lady's Book*, an influential women's magazine in the nineteenth century, decreed: "Custom has decided, from the earliest ages, that white is the most fitting hue, whatever may be the material. It is an emblem of the purity and innocence of girlhood, and the unsullied heart she now yields to the chosen one."

These days, anything goes—but white remains the color of choice for most brides. The grooms, after all, wouldn't want it any other way. Take it from Billy Idol.

Q Why do strippers and barbers have their own poles?

A Yes, strippers and barbers have something in common. And if that notion has produced a gruesome image in your head of Floyd the Barber gyrating to Mötley Crüe's "Girls, Girls, Girls," we apologize.

Both professions can be quickly identified by a single object: a pole. There is, of course, at least one notable difference: The barber pole sits outside the place of employment, whereas the stripper pole is the place of employment. How did these poles come to be, anyway?

We'll start with the barber pole. In addition to cutting hair and shaving faces, barbers in fifteenth-century England were the town medical professionals. When someone was sick, he or she went to the barber for a bloodletting, a common way to treat illnesses back then.

Why the barber? Well, he was the guy in town with the sharp blades. Patients would come in, grab a pole tightly so that their veins would show, and let the barber cut their arms and bleed them until they fainted. After the procedure, the bloodstained bandages were hung on a pole outside to dry—and to advertise the special business. In the wind, the crimson and white bandages would wrap themselves around the pole in a spiral pattern.

Does the pattern sound familiar? Blood-stained white cloths were eventually replaced with red and white paint, and the pole became a more tasteful marketing tool. While barbers weren't doing much bloodletting by the end of the eighteenth century, the striped pole remained a permanent fixture in front of shops in America and Europe. Today, a barber pole is synonymous with a haircut, a shave, and some good conversation.

A shiny brass pole in a bar conjures a different sort of image: that of a scantily clad woman, one whose name ends in "i" or "y," swinging around to the suggestive beat of a hair-metal band. The idea of combining a woman with a pole dates back more than a century. Traveling burlesque shows in the early twentieth century added strip tease dances to entice men to return the next time the act was in town. The shows often took place in tents, and some of the dancers would hold on to a tent pole to dance around; they would use the pole to gain leverage for the high kicks that always drew cheers from the men sitting in the front.

By the 1980s, pole-dancing was a staple in exotic bars. Today, the stripper pole has gained mainstream acceptance—it is even used as a popular exercise tool. Fitness clubs throughout the United States offer pole-dancing workouts (the women are, of course, clothed in this variation), and poles are available for purchase by those who want to tone up at home. There are even pole-dancing fitness competitions, in which participants combine gymnastic moves with choreographed dance routines.

Sadly, these competitions don't feature a division for barbers. Sorry, Floyd.

Q Why is the heart associated with love?

A Who doesn't eagerly await Valentine's Day? It's a day to celebrate your true love in the name of Saint Valentine, the patron saint of lovers. That Valentine became a saint by being beaten, stoned, and beheaded is rarely considered. Unless you're in a really bad relationship, Valentine's Day is not about beheadings, but about hearts: heart-shaped flower arrangements, heart-shaped cards, heart-shaped balloons, heart-shaped boxes of chocolates, and heart-shaped candies that taste like chalk. Hearts. Hearts everywhere. There's no escaping the hearts.

Since the time of the ancient Greeks, people have associated the heart organ with love. Aristotle posited that affections were housed in the human heart. But how did the heart shape become so ubiquitous, not only on Valentine's Day but in relation to anything associated with love? Think about it for a moment—does the ♥ symbol really look anything like a human heart? Not unless you have some serious cardiac issues. In fact, the heart shape now associated with love may not have had anything to do with hearts in the first place.

There are a couple of explanations for the origin of the symbol. The first has its roots in the ancient city of Cyrene, a Greek colony located in what is now Libya. Archeologists unearthed silver coins used in Cyrene that were stamped with the shape of the seed of a now-extinct plant, silphium.

The plant was important to ancient Cyrenians—silphium was used as a contraceptive. Interestingly, the seed's depiction is almost identical to the contemporary ♥ shape associated with love. This theory holds that the use of the plant, coupled with the prevalence of its image on circulating money, led to a natural marriage of the heart shape with love (or, at least, with passion).

This is an intriguing explanation, but like many stories of origin, it may not be entirely accurate. More likely, the development of the heart symbol is a slower, less racy tale. In fact, the heart symbol may have its roots in ivy-leaf motifs found in ancient art. Pottery and frescoes unearthed from ancient Minos, Crete, and Afghanistan all show prominent use of the heart-shaped ivy leaf. This motif was borrowed by later artists, including religious painters and sculptors, who incorporated the heart shape into depictions of Jesus and Mary as symbols of pure, unconditional love.

Once the Sacred Heart devotion of Catholicism co-opted the symbol in the Middle Ages, it became more popularly associated with love. Shortly afterward, the heart became a standard suit on playing cards, and soon the symbol was integrated into depictions of courtly love.

When the first Valentine's Day was celebrated in the late fifth century, it was only natural to associate the heart symbol with the lovers' day. Now the heart symbol is forever linked with romantic love, relegating future generations to an onslaught of heart-shaped kitsch.

Chapter Three

ORIGINS AND TRADITIONS

Q **Are hatters more prone to go mad than regular folk?**

A For a long time, hatters had the unfortunate reputation of being off their rockers. It was not uncommon to see a man of this trade walking alone down the street, mum-bling to himself, sometimes shaking with uncontrollable jitters. The sight was so ubiquitous, the phenomenon so mysterious—and so specific to the trade—that the *New York Times* published an article in 1880 speculating that it was a congenital lunacy that drove a man to this profession in the first place.

To top it off, if you'll excuse the pun, the phrase "mad as a hatter" had begun appearing in literature as early as 1850 before being driven home in 1865, when Lewis Carroll introduced the world to the Mad Hatter in his book *Alice's Adventures in Wonderland.* So how did hatters come into such a reputation?

If you'll excuse another pun, it boils down to the use of mercury in their work. Hatters toiled in small, poorly ventilated rooms—such were the labor conditions of the era—with a pot of mercurous nitrate literally on the burner at all times. The solution softened and matted the pelts they used in making their hats, which were mostly comprised of rabbit and beaver. Breathing toxic mercury fumes for hours on end, day after day, caused extensive brain damage in these men. In other words, the longer they worked as hatters, the madder they became.

The symptoms of brain damage caused by mercury fumes include drooling, loss of memory, tremors, and psychotic behavior—all of which combine into the figure seen walking down the street, mumbling to himself. The hatter is truly a tragic figure, destroyed by his desire to cap the capless. And, if Lewis Carroll can be believed, the eventual outcome of this madness is a never-ending tea party with a Dormouse and a March Hare and the celebration, 364 days out of the year, of one's "un-birthday."

Use of the chemical dwindled until the mid-1960s, when the pot of mercury was taken off the burner for good. Its use for manufacturing purposes was outlawed, but the damage had already been done. A large amount of mercury had contaminated the lands upon which the hatters' workhouses stood. The chemical then seeped into the ground, rivers, and lakes. What's in the lakes is in the fish, and what's in the fish, to some extent, is in our bodies. (Fear of mercury is what makes doctors caution pregnant women against eating fish.) Government agencies are still studying the effects this has had on the environment.

Since mercury is no longer allowed, modern hatmakers achieve a similar effect using sandpaper. Mercurous nitrate was used to slick the pelt down; turns out a rough massage with a quarter sheet of the proper grit does the job just as well—and without the brain damage. Too bad we couldn't have gleaned this information sooner. It would have prevented many a hatter from going mad.

Q Why are barns usually painted red?

A Barns usually are the largest and most recognizable structures in rural areas. Barns stand out not only because of their unique configuration, but also because most are painted red or white, two of the brightest colors in the spectrum. But back when the first barns were raised in North America, picking a pretty color wasn't exactly a part of the design process. Practicality and penny-pinching were the priorities, and barns ended up being predominantly red pretty much by accident.

European farmers were the first to paint their barns, using a mixture of lime, linseed oil, and milk. This combination was cost-effective and made an excellent paint that protected the barn's wood from the harsh elements. However, the mixture didn't protect against mold and moss, which decayed the wood. Farmers added ferric oxide (rust), an antidecaying agent, to the paint, and the mixture took on a rusty red color.

This cheap but effective red-paint mixture was so popular that red barns began popping up all over Europe. European settlers brought their red paint with them to North America, and they continued to slap it on their barns long after factory-mixed paints became available. Why? Red paint was still cheap and durable in the nineteenth century, and most farmers preferred to stick with tradition.

White is the second-most popular color for barns. Dairy farmers, in particular, favor white because it stands for cleanliness and purity, which are traits they want associated with the milk from their cows.

Q Why is 666 the sign of the Devil?

A No, this question wasn't lifted from an Iron Maiden song. Like most reliable information on the subject, the connection between the Devil and the number 666 comes from the Bible. And if you were a regular at Sunday school, you might rightfully suspect that the explanation originates from the zaniest book of the Bible, the Book of Revelation.

The New Testament saved most of its craziness for its final act, in which we see Satan rise to power and destroy the world, only to have Christ come back and pulverize him at the last second. In chapter thirteen (how's that for spooky?) of the book, we learn that an integral part of Satan's power-grab is sending an emissary to Earth who will force its inhabitants to worship the Devil. The chapter goes on to say that all who pledge allegiance to this emissary must wear his mark on their hands or foreheads or else risk getting shut out of the new evil-topia.

Finally, at verse eighteen, we get this tidbit (depending on your translation): "Wisdom is needed here; one who understands can calculate the number of the beast, for it is a number that stands for a person. His number is six hundred and sixty-six." Thus, the number of both the Devil and the Antichrist is revealed to be 666.

Many people have noted that this fact is unusually specific for a book that otherwise deals with what are presumably symbols, such as dragons coming out of the earth and fire shooting from the sky. As with the interpretation of the Book of Revelation in general, there has been a lot of debate about the precise meaning of this number.

On one side, there is the lunatic fringe, which ascribes the sign of the beast to whichever public figure has raised its ire. In the 1980s, for example, some malcontents pointed out that President Reagan's full name—Ronald Wilson Reagan—is composed of three six-letter groupings.

A more sane theory attributes the number 666 to the Roman emperor Nero. Nero blamed the Christians for the infamous burning of Rome in the first century AD, and consequently started a brutal campaign of persecution against the fledgling religion. It is believed that the author of the Book of Revelation, John the Apostle, was attempting to send a coded message to his fellow Christians to give them hope that Nero's tyranny would soon come to an end.

To ensure that only other Christians would understand his message, John used Hebrew numerology. John chose Hebrew because it is the language of Judaism, the religion that Christianity grew out of after the arrival of Christ. In Hebrew, each letter corresponds with a number. The letters/numbers from Nero's full name in Hebrew, Neron Qeisar, add up to—you guessed it—666.

Essentially, John was telling his readers that Nero would be deposed, the persecution of the Christians would end, and that Christ would return to start the Rapture. We're still waiting on John's third prediction to come true, but as a lesser light, Meatloaf, once said, "Two out of three ain't bad."

Q Why don't cars have hood ornaments anymore?

A Stand-up hood ornaments, or "mascots," as they are known in Britain, faded almost completely from automobile hoods in the early 1970s. They succumbed to the realities of fuel-saving aerodynamics, pedestrian safety, styling trends, and plain old cost cutting.

It was the close of a tradition that began with function and ended with fantasy.

The earliest hood ornaments were literally a decorative outgrowth of a small metal cap that contained a temperature gauge; the cap was screwed onto the filler neck of a car's radiator. The upright frame and mesh covering of the exposed radiator was a fixture of car design from the dawn of the motorized age in the late nineteenth century into the 1930s. Automakers seized an opportunity to treat the cap as a ready-made pedestal to promote an image. For example, radiator caps in the 1910s and 1920s frequently took the shape of a silken-robed woman, often winged, to suggest an aura of quiet refinement that contrasted with the noisy, smoky cars of the day.

Locomotives were a common hood-ornament theme in the 1930s, as automakers sought a link to the power and modernity of the streamlined age. By the 1940s, cars had enclosed their radiators and filler caps within stylized grilles, and gauges had moved inside the car to the dashboard, but the hood ornament remained a strong symbol; ornaments in the shape of torpedoes and gun sights reflected the wartime bravado. Jet-age motifs took over in the 1950s, with chromed aircraft and rocket shapes that were a fitting bookend for the tailfins of the day. Some automakers viewed the hood ornament not as metaphor, but as advertisement. DeSoto, for example, used a bust of its namesake, the Spanish explorer, complete with helmet and armor.

By the late 1960s, stand-up hood ornaments had become code for certain old-fashioned values, and makes like Lincoln, Oldsmobile, and Cadillac were among the few that continued to display them. They didn't have a place on cars that were aimed at the youth market. But practical concerns also played a role in their demise, as automakers sought to cut down on wind resistance in the name of better fuel economy, to eliminate a danger to a person struck by a car, and to use less-expensive molded plastic or a thin stamped-metal insignia glued to a hood or grille.

Today, only select cars have stand-up hood ornaments. One is the Rolls-Royce, with its elegant female figure, known as "The Flying Lady" in the Unites States and "Spirit of Ecstasy" in Britain. Even she has bowed to modern realities: The lady is spring-loaded to withdraw instantaneously at the slightest impact; as an anti-theft measure, she can also be retracted by the driver with the push of a dashboard button.

Q How many idiots owned a Pet Rock?

A At least 1.3 million by Christmas morning, 1975. And watch who you're calling an idiot!

That figure counts only the original Pet Rocks. In the months before Christmas, thousands of cheaper imitations were also sold, and no one can guess how many of those changed hands.

Gary Dahl, the marketing genius who thought up the Pet Rock, got the idea from listening to his friends complain about their troublesome pets. He persuaded a former boss to back him financially and arranged to haul two and a half tons of pebbles from Rosarita Beach in Mexico to his Northern California headquarters. After packaging them in carrying crates filled with nesting straw and cut with air holes, he introduced the Pet Rock at gift shows that autumn.

Soon he was shipping thousands of rocks per day to stores such as Neiman-Marcus and Macy's. Dahl earned ninety-five cents for every authentic Pet Rock sold at $3.95. He became a million-aire three weeks before Christmas, appeared on TV talk shows, and was written up in *Newsweek, People*, and many major news-papers.

Why? What sparked such an insane fad? Dahl took a stab at ex-plaining it, saying, "I think the country was depressed and need-ed a giggle." He was probably right, because for most people, the real fun of having a Pet Rock was reading the manual. Written by Dahl and titled *The Care and Training of Your PET ROCK*, the thirty-two-page booklet described how to teach your new pet basic commands such as "Stay," "Sit," and "Play dead." Although rocks learned these tricks quickly, more complicated commands such as "Come" required "extraordinary patience" from the trainer.

Nostalgic attempts to recreate the magic, or take it a step further with Rock Concerts or Rock Families (often with googly eyes glued onto the rocks), fell flat. In 2000, Pet Rocks were packaged and sold with minimal changes to the original design. One no-ticeable omission in the 2000 version of the manual was the "At-tack" command. In 1975, owners were told that when confronted by a mugger, they should, "Reach into your pocket or purse [and] extract your pet rock. Shout the command, ATTACK. And bash the mugger's head in." Presumably, the twenty-first century is too litigious to give this advice to rock owners.

None of the redux sales strategies worked. Pet Rocks enjoyed their fifteen minutes of fame, but after their initial—and legendary—success, all attempts to remarket Pet Rocks have dropped like a stone.

Q Do atheists have to swear on the Bible in court?

A Technically, atheists do not have to swear on the Bible in court. The same goes for agnostics, Buddhists, Gothics, Mormons, Jews, Quakers, Wiccans, Muslims, or any Christian who decides to step out of line. Come on, it *could* happen. Not one single citizen of the United States, no matter what his or her religion, has to swear on the Bible when taking the oath in court, thanks to a Supreme Court ruling saying that the "government may not require a person to swear to any belief he or she does not hold. Witnesses have the option of affirming that they will tell the truth, without reference to the Bible or God."

Where exactly did this Bible-God-oath tradition come from? The word "oath" is Anglo-Saxon in origin, and its meaning is pretty straightforward. An oath is defined as a solemn promise, words of promise, or a swear word. Swearing on the Bible was traditional back in England, where witnesses swore before God—and actually kissed the Bible. But it is important to note that until around the mid-seventeenth century, only Christians had any standing in court. Atheists and those who didn't believe that God punished wrongdoers were disqualified from acting as witnesses under the common law rule.

This is where the word technically comes into play. Back in the seventeenth century, atheists and nonbelievers could be legally disqualified from acting as witnesses under the common law rule. Today, it is against the law to disqualify an atheist from acting as a witness, but it is no secret that he or she can be disqualified in the minds of judges and jurors.

So no, atheists do not have to swear on the Bible in court. They can affirm instead by simply answering "yes" to the following question: "You do affirm that all the testimony you are about to give in the case now before the court will be the truth, the whole truth, and nothing but the truth; this you do affirm under the pains and penalties of perjury?" But doing so in the United States, which has the largest Christian population on the earth (78.5 percent), will probably raise more than just an eyebrow.

Q Why do people knock on wood for good luck?

A Finally, things seem to be going right. When you comment on that fact, however, you have an irresistible urge to add the phrase "knock on wood" and frantically seek out the nearest table, desk, chair, or doorjamb so that you can rap your knuckles on it a few times for good luck. But why is it good luck?

Many people point to the rosary as the origin of the "knock on wood" phenomenon. Rosaries, or "prayer beads," are a series of wooden beads strung together, often with some sort of religious icon, usually a wooden crucifix, where the two ends join. In times of prayer, Christians rub the rosary beads. The tradition dates back to at least the fourth century, when Christians flocked to Constantinople to touch the cross on which Jesus was believed to have been crucified—it was thought that this artifact would bestow blessings and healing upon those who touched it. Pilgrims would touch the cross three times, in deference to the Christian Holy Trinity; this practice eventually evolved into a series of shorter, faster motions, leading to the "knocking" of today.

Another religious theory comes from the pagan notion of nature spirits. By knocking on wood, one is thought to invoke the protection of the spirits that reside within the wood. Some even go so far as to knock only on the underside of a table or other piece of furniture, believing that to do otherwise is to bop the spirit on the head, which is not very polite at all and could serve to anger the spirit.

And then there's the mundane suggestion that knocking on wood for good luck stems from a simple game of tag. *The Boy's Own Book*, published in England in 1829, lays out the rules of this now-ubiquitous playground game: A wooden (or iron, in some versions) post or a tree is designated as a "safe spot," and anyone who touches it is immune from being tagged. Some of us never grew out of that notion, and to this day, when things go south, we seek the "safety" of nearby wooden objects.

However it got here, by 1908 the phrase had entered American lexicon. An article in the *Indianapolis Star* that year used the phrase at least twice, in its familiar, modern form. The article focused on a promising young athlete, and the author took care to add the parenthetical phrase "knock on wood!" after assertions of the athlete's potential prowess. No word on whether these embellishments helped propel the athlete to greatness.

Q Are there cultures in which a woman can have multiple husbands?

A When someone mentions polygamy, we usually think of certain Mormon fundamentalists or Muslim sects that allow a man to have multiple wives. Anthropologists use the term "polygamy" to refer to any marriage system that involves more than two people. The "one husband, many wives" form is called "polygyny." The "one wife, multiple husbands" version is called "polyandry." And if anthropologists have a special word for it, it must exist somewhere.

Polyandry is, however, exceedingly rare. Only a few cultures continue to practice it today, and polyandry is gradually being eroded by more modern ideas of love and marriage. The strongholds of polyandry are Tibet, Nepal, and certain parts of India, and it is also practiced in Sri Lanka. Other cultures were polyandrous in the past, though it was never widespread.

In many cases, this marriage practice takes the form of fraternal polyandry, in which one woman is married to several brothers. There may be a primary husband, the eldest brother or the first one she married. If additional brothers are born after the marriage, they usually become the woman's husbands as well.

The reasons for polyandry are typically more economic than religious. In the areas where it is practiced, life is difficult and poverty is rampant. If a family divided its property among all the brothers, no one would have enough land to survive on through farming and herding. Keeping all the brothers as part of one family keeps the familial plot in one piece. The herding lifestyle also means one or more brothers are often away tending the livestock for extended periods, so the other husbands can stay at home, protect the family, and tend the farm. Where resources are so limited, polyandry also serves as a form of birth control, since the wife can only get pregnant once every nine months no matter how many husbands she has.

No one is ever sure which father sired which child, so each tends to treat all of the kids as if they are his own. Do the husbands get jealous? Certainly. Do the wives get tired of providing sex for many husbands? Sure, but this final point is universal. Many wives with just one husband get tired of providing sex, too.

Q Why do priests wear white collars?

A It seems we've stumbled upon one of the hot topics in the clerical blogosphere. (Who even knew there was a clerical blogosphere?) It's actually not just Catholic priests who sport these circular signifiers, but also pastors in the Lutheran, Episcopal, Anglican, and some other Christian and Pentecostal churches. There's even the odd Buddhist or Baptist who puts one on. The debate centers on how lay society reacts to this white collar. Some men—and women—of the cloth say it is a well-known symbol of holiness that makes them more approachable; others contend that it connotes a certain formality and rigidity that has just the opposite effect.

Either way, the white collar is a remaining portion of what was once a more extensive ensemble. In the earliest days, the business of the church was probably conducted in regular day-to-day clothing. The idea that clergy should wear special garments separating them from secular life seems to have emerged in the fourth century, around the time the Emperor Constantine converted to Christianity and brought the Roman Empire with him. Since then, those performing sacraments and leading Mass have worn liturgical vestments.

In the Middle Ages, to keep the clergy from succumbing to extravagance and to make them easily identifiable outside the walls of the sanctuary, popes instructed priests to dress modestly and simply, usually in a plain black tunic or a cassock. The ensuing years saw other popes exert their influence on priestly fashion, as well. In 1589, for instance, Pope Sixtus V prescribed penalties for priests who failed to wear cassocks. Clement XI loosened things up a bit in 1708, authorizing a shorter, more convenient travel jacket for priests to wear on the road. Seventeen years later, Pope Benedict XIII put his holy foot down and nixed civilian attire altogether.

The Code of Canon Law, which lays out the rules of the Catholic Church, notes that "clerics are to wear suitable ecclesiastical garb according to the norms issued by the conference of bishops and according to legitimate local customs." The trademark component of this ecclesiastical garb is the white collar. One colorful version of the origin of the Roman collar suggests that the slick, detachable number worn today was invented in the late eighteen hundreds by the Scottish—and non-Catholic—Rev. Dr. Donald McLeod. But the inspiration likely came from the Catholic Church's Roman collarino, which had evolved in the sixteen hundreds as a means for priests to keep their black cassock collars clean and also mimicked a popular folded-collar style. A narrow band of linen covered the neckband and could be removed for laundering as needed. So practical! Now sure, white shows dirt more readily than black, but the collar also symbolizes obedience to God, so its pure whiteness—not to mention the challenge of keeping it that way—enhanced the overall effect.

Given the strides we've made with laundering techniques in the past few centuries, those currently encased in the collar report that its purpose has more to do with helping the wearers remember their service and responsibilities, and reminding the lay population that God is present in the world. As Rev. Antonio Hernández, an American Buddhist priest who wears the collar, says, "One has no choice but to guard one's behavior while strapped into one of these."

Q Why do people wear costumes on Halloween?

A Why do we deck ourselves out like Spider-Man or the Wicked Witch of the West on Halloween? When you think about it, it's a pretty silly way to celebrate the eve of All Saints' Day. Turns out that dressing in masks and costumes started along with trick-or-treating about three hundred and fifty years ago.

The earliest mention of wearing disguises on Halloween comes from Ireland and Scotland in the seventeenth century. In small villages and rural areas, folks dressed up in costumes and got rowdy. Why? Well, since the first few centuries of the Christian era, Halloween in those Celtic lands had a reputation of being the night when ghosts, witches, demons, and faeries were free to wander. That made it the perfect time to get away with a bit of mischief-making. People also wore masks to avoid being recognized by the wandering ghosts. Men and boys hid behind masks or rubbed charcoal all over their faces, then ran around making noise, throwing trash, and harassing their neighbors (playing tricks, in other words). Sometimes they chased pretty girls or went begging for gifts (the treats). Girls joined in the fun on occasion, always in disguise. But mostly it was a night of male bonding, showing off, and trying to outdo each other.

By the end of the nineteenth century, more than two million men and women had emigrated from Ireland to live in North American cities. Quite naturally, they tended to live near other Irish families in the same neighborhoods, and they celebrated the holidays the way they had in the Old Country. On Halloween, that meant dressing up in disguises and running around, dumping trash in the streets or begging for gifts. Among more genteel families, it meant costume parties—a practice that quickly became popular with all city folks.

In the United States, it didn't take long for storekeepers to realize they could make a profit off this curious custom. By the late eighteen hundreds, shops were selling masks throughout October for children and adults. By the twentieth century, Halloween was celebrated coast to coast, and families, schools, and churches all hosted costume parties. The first citywide Halloween celebration happened in Anoka, Minnesota, in 1921.

The long-term result? Halloween is big business. About 60 percent of all Americans celebrate Halloween, and one-third of them bought costumes in 2007. Those people each spent an average of about thirty-eight dollars on their fancy frocks—for a total of $1.82 billion.

Q Why is Friday the thirteenth unlucky?

A It's perhaps the most pervasive superstition in North America, Western Europe, and Australia. In fact, if you're like lots of other fearful folks, you won't take a flight, get married, sign a contract, or even leave your house on this most doomed of days.

What exactly makes Friday the thirteenth more luckless than, say, Tuesday the fifth? The answer is deeply rooted in biblical, mythological, and historical events.

Friday and the number thirteen have been independently sinister since ancient times—maybe since the dawn of humans. Many biblical scholars say that Eve tempted Adam with the forbidden apple on a Friday. Traditional teachings also tell us that the Great Flood began on a Friday, the Temple of Solomon was destroyed on a Friday, and Abel was slain by Cain on a Friday.

For Christians, Friday and the number thirteen are of the utmost significance. Christ was crucified on Friday, and thirteen is the number of people who were present at the Last Supper. Judas, the disciple who betrayed Jesus, was the thirteenth member of the party to arrive.

Groups of thirteen may be one of the earliest and most concrete taboos associated with the number. It's believed that both the ancient Vikings and Hindus thought it unpropitious to have thirteen people gather together in one place. Up until recently, French socialites known as *quatorziens* (fourteeners) made themselves available as fourteenth guests to spare dinner parties from ominous ends.

Some trace the infamy of the number thirteen back to ancient Norse culture. According to mythology, twelve gods were invited to a banquet, when in walked an uninvited thirteenth guest— Loki, the god of mischief. Loki tricked the blind god Hod into throwing a spear of mistletoe at Balder, the beloved god of light. Balder fell dead, and the whole Earth turned dark.

In modern times, thirteen continues to be a number to avoid. About 80 percent of high-rise buildings don't have a thirteenth floor, many airports skip gate number thirteen, and you won't find a room thirteen in some hospitals and hotels.

How did Friday and thirteen become forever linked as the most disquieting day on the calendar? It just may be that Friday was unlucky and thirteen was unlucky, so a combination of the two was simply a double jinx. However, one theory holds that all this superstition came not as a result of convergent taboos, but of a single historical event.

On Friday, October 13, 1307, King Philip IV of France ordered the arrest of the revered Knights Templars. Tortured and forced to confess to false charges of heresy, blasphemy, and wrongdoing, hundreds of knights were burned at the stake. It's said that sympathizers of the Templars then condemned Friday the thirteenth as the most evil of days.

No one has been able to document if this eerie tale is indeed the origin of the Friday the thirteenth superstition. And really, some scholars are convinced that it's nothing more than a phenomenon created by twentieth-century media. So sufferers of paraskevidekatriaphobia (a pathological fear of Friday the thirteenth), take some comfort—or at least throw some salt over your shoulder.

Q Why is it considered bad luck to walk under a ladder?

A It's not just bad luck to walk under a ladder—it's an all-around bad practice. Even the most ardent skeptics, those who pay no mind to a black cat or a newly cracked mirror, recognize the practical danger inherent in ducking under a ladder. Three words can sum it up: open paint can. Who knows what might be precariously balanced atop the highest step (the "Not a Step" step)? One wrong move and you might find yourself showered with Cinnamon Speckle Semi-Gloss.

But what about the superstitious aversion to ladders? This goes back at least as far as the sixteen hundreds. In this period, the theory goes, when the condemned were being led to the gallows to be hanged, they were forced to walk under the ladder that led to the last platform their boots would ever be planted on; the executioner, meanwhile, walked around it. This ritual, witnessed weekly by an enthralled mass of people, brought about the association of everyday ladders with death in general and the gallows in particular. For the average person, walking under a ladder was the same as tempting fate, invoking his or her own death.

Another theory has the triangular shape formed by a ladder leaning against a building representing the Christian Trinity—the Father, Son, and Holy Spirit. Breaking a triangle, which was thought to be sacred, was considered blasphemous; defying God in such a way was tantamount to declaring an allegiance with the Devil. People avoided walking under ladders to keep their friends and neighbors from thinking they had made such a pact. In times when the popular vote could get a man hanged for alleged involvement in witchcraft and other devilry, quashing such rumors before they started might have been a matter of life and death.

At any rate, skeptics and believers alike should be cautious when confronted with a ladder. Whether the outcome is an eternity in Hell or an afternoon washing latex paint out of your hair, taking a few extra steps around a ladder seems like a small price to pay for personal safety.

Q How do generations get their names?

A In The Who's 1965 song "My Generation," lead singer Roger Daltrey famously declared that he hoped he'd die before he got old. But what exactly was Daltrey's generation? For starters, it didn't die. Instead, it got old, giving us, among other mediocrities, minivans along the way. We know the people from this generation as Baby Boomers.

Agreeing on a name for a generation is tricky business. Equally tricky is figuring out exactly who belongs to which generation. (There is no official Council of Generation Naming.) If it's a problem, though, it's a fairly recent one. It is only with the rise of *en masse* self-consciousness—and rampant narcissism—that people have even cared about naming generations.

Historically, generations have gotten their names from literary sources. One of the first generations to name itself was the Generation of '98, a movement of Spanish artists and writers who pointed to the Spanish-American War of 1898 as a break from an artistic and political past. The generational term Baby Boomer was coined in a 1974 *Time* magazine article about Bob Dylan. And Generation X, though around for some time beforehand, was cemented in the popular mind by Douglas Coupland's eponymous 1991 novel.

Possibly the most famous and influential—and certainly the most romantic—generation of the twentieth century was known as the Lost Generation. The term is attributed to writer Gertrude Stein, who used it to describe disillusioned World War I veterans. Stein's cohorts in Paris, among them Ernest Hemingway, embraced the term. Of course, critics are quick to point out that a few artists and expatriates traipsing about the Left Bank hardly qualify as an entire generation. Which points to the futility of such an exercise in generalization in the first place.

Historians William Strauss and Neil Howe created an entire history around generational movements. Naturally, Strauss and Howe made an effort to name some generations themselves. (Some of their names include the rather inspired 13th Generation for the group everybody else calls Generation X, and the silly Homeland Generation for the current generational crop.) As of late, the desire for satisfactory generation names has reached a fevered pitch, with no fewer than five monikers being bandied about for the current generation. (Thankfully, it appears Howe and Strauss's Homeland Generation is gaining little traction.)

As we said, most generations have been anointed by literary critics, writers, and other intellectual types. So it is perhaps bleak testimony to the era we live in that Generation Y—the most widely recognized term for the generation following Generation X—was dubbed so by the magazine *Advertising Age*.

Q What's the difference between Cajun and Creole?

A This is a question to ponder the next time you're stumbling down Bourbon Street after a long night of Mardi Gras revelry.

Once, on a visit to a Louisiana bayou, an old Cajun said to us: "I got an ahnvee for some chee wee." We have no idea what that means, but such phrases are part of what makes Cajun culture—its language, its accordion-heavy music, and its crawfish étouffée—an integral part of the romance of New Orleans. The history of Louisiana Cajuns goes back to the French and Indian War of the mid-eighteenth century, when England and France battled over large swaths of colonial land, including what was then known as Acadia (now part of Nova Scotia, Canada).

Though Acadia was at that time part of a British colony, it was populated mostly by French settlers. Wary of having a colony full of French people during an impending war with France, the Brits kicked out everyone of French descent. These displaced settlers scattered all over North America, but a large percentage of them headed down to another French colony, Louisiana.

Though New Orleans was at that time a thriving port community, Acadians instead settled in the surrounding swampy, alligator-infested bayou regions. Through the years, the Acadians, or Cajuns, as they came to be known, developed a close-knit, if isolated, community with its own dialect, music, and folk wisdom. Technically, only people who are descended from the communities settled by those original displaced Acadians are considered Cajun.

Creole, on the other hand, can refer to any number of things. Originally the term, which dates back to the Spanish conquest of Latin America, meant any person descended from colonial settlers; eventually, any people of mixed race who were native to the colonies became known as Creoles. To add further confusion to the definition, there is something called a Creole language, which is most often born of the contact between a colonial language and a native one.

In Louisiana, Creole refers to people of any race born in Louisiana who descended from the original French settlers of the colony. These folks differ from Cajuns in that they came from places other than Acadia. Louisianan Creoles, too, have their own language—which differs from Cajun—that blends French, West African, and Native American languages; music (such as zydeco); and cuisine.

So there you have it—the difference between Cajun and Creole. Now you can think about something else the next time you're staggering down Bourbon Street—like how you're going to get rid of all the beads you've collected before you return home to your spouse.

Q Why do we toast by clinking glasses?

A There was nothing like a few libations to get the questions flowing for this book. Unfortunately, those questions usually wound up being something along the lines of, "Whose pants are these, and why am I wearing them on my head?" But on one occasion—after our tenth or eleventh toast—we wondered just why we were clinking our glasses together. Hey, a legitimate question!

As is often the case with matters such as this, there is the interesting explanation and then there is the real one. For many years, the dominant theory held that clinking glasses after a toast was not a sign of friendship, but of mistrust. Back in ancient times, when poisoning was the preferred method of dispatching one's enemies, a host would clink glasses with his guests, making sure they sloshed a little vino into each other's cups to prove that the wine was not poisoned. This theory has been largely discredited. Besides the logistical nightmare (not to mention the cleaning bill) of trying to get wine into other people's cups without spilling, it seems unlikely that ancient social events were so perpetually treacherous that this would evolve into a common social custom.

To understand why we clink glasses after a toast, we need to examine where the custom of toasting began. It does seem a little strange, after all—we don't thrust our food-laden forks into the air and offer syrupy platitudes before taking the first bite of a meal. Then again, in the Western tradition, eating from the same plate doesn't have quite the same history that drinking from the same cup does.

Indeed, many historians identify toasting's origins in the drinking habits of the ancient Greeks. In those heady, wine-filled days, it was customary for groups of acquaintances to share the same drinking vessel. The host would take the first sip and then pass the cup to the next person in the party, often accompanying this gesture with a pleasantry or a wish for good health. As the centuries passed, drinking, though still a largely communal act, no longer involved a collective drinking vessel. So clinking became popular, to provide the communal sense once afforded by a shared vessel.

Why do we call it a "toast"? In medieval British times, people drank whatever they could get their hands on. The Brits, never known for their culinary expertise, didn't produce the finest wines and spirits, and to make their sometimes acidic quaffs more palatable, on occasion they would drop a piece of spiced, charred bread into the drink. (Charcoal has anti-acidic properties.) Shakespeare fans will surely remember Falstaff, possibly the most glorious drunk of all time, demanding a "quart of sack" with "toast in't" in *The Merry Wives of Windsor*.

There is another interesting, if questionable, theory about toasting that bears mentioning. It's been suggested that clinking glasses derives from the medieval belief that alcohol was possessed by demons. Medieval folks thought that loud noises would drive demons away, and so a clinking of the glasses prior to imbibing would inhibit the evil spirits from making you do bad things. This theory has been discredited, but the idea of evil spirits inhabiting alcohol has continued to the present day. Indeed, we've tried this excuse ourselves. Trust us, it doesn't work.

Q Why do people say "bless you" when someone sneezes?

A A sneeze—*sternutation* is the medical term for it—is acknowledged in many different languages. In Arabic, for example, a polite person says *alhamdu lillah* ("praise be to

God") when someone sneezes. If you speak Telugu, you'll say *chiranjeeva*, which means "live for an eternity." In German, g*esundheit* is the usual response to an "achoo!" It's *jai mati ji* in Hindi, and *na zdrowie* in Polish. Yet there isn't a routine comment to reply to belching, farting, coughing, snoring, or having one's joints creak. Why sneezing?

If you think about it, sneezing is an odd reflex. It even appears to border on the perilous. Anthropologists guess that prehistoric man might well have acknowledged a sneeze as a means of giving thanks that the person had been given another chance at life. The sneezer's breath, and very essence, had abruptly exploded from the body, but the breath immediately after the sneeze restored life, something to be thankful for.

What about modern society, specifically the English-speaking segment? Why do people say "bless you" after someone sneezes? There are many theories, and a prominent one has its roots in Rome. (Doesn't everything?) In AD 590, Pope Gregory I asked for unending prayers by the people and for chanting priests to parade through the streets in hopes of warding off an epidemic of bubonic plague.

Sneezing was considered an early symptom of the disease, and the "bless you" was meant to ask for the blessings of God. That might not have been a bad idea even if modern theories of disease transmission hadn't yet developed—a sneeze can spray thousands of bacteria-filled droplets. Which is why we customarily cover our mouths when we sneeze.

Sneezing isn't dangerous. Some people even find it pleasurable enough to use snuff, or ground tobacco, to induce sneezing.

The urban myth that your eyes will pop out of your head if you sneeze with your eyes open is just that—an urban myth. Scientists aren't sure why people reflexively close their eyes when they sneeze, but there's no evidence that your eyes will pop out if you hold them open. So sneeze away—someone undoubtedly will be waiting to wish you well.

Chapter Four

BODY SCIENCE

Q Why do pregnant women crave pickles?

A Countless women have successfully brought a baby to term without eating a single pickle, which is one reason why the topic of pregnancy cravings is controversial. No one is exactly sure how many women experience this phenomenon. Some studies say roughly half of pregnant women develop some sort of food craving, while other research puts the number as high as 80 percent. Regardless, the more pertinent question is: Why do some pregnant women get food cravings?

The so-called experts aren't much help. Some physicians attribute these cravings to nothing more than the expectant mother seeking comfort food. A woman, the thinking goes, may attempt to ease the anxiety of pregnancy with such soothing tastes as ice cream or chocolate (which has been shown to stimulate the release of endorphins).

But what about pickles? One research group has postulated that food cravings during pregnancy are the result of a mineral deficiency in a woman's body. Because a mother-to-be's blood volume nearly doubles during pregnancy, it is possible that the nutrient distribution in her bloodstream can become diluted. As a result, a pregnant woman might unconsciously seek out certain foods to restore this balance. If the woman's body is running low on sodium, for example, she might crack open a jar of pickles, which are soaked in a sodium-filled brine.

This theory seems perfectly logical, but there isn't much evidence to back it up. For instance, the American Academy of Pediatrics reports that a lot of kids don't have enough calcium in their diets, but when was the last time you saw a child pass up a soda for a glass of milk?

The most popular theory centers on a factor to which men ascribe to any inexplicable female behavior: raging hormones. It's a fact that the avalanche of hormones released during pregnancy causes a number of discomforts, such as fatigue, swelling, headaches, and mood swings. Does the list sound familiar? It should. It contains the same discomforts many women experience during their "time of the month."

In the second half of the menstrual cycle, the levels of estrogen and progesterone begin to rise, just as they do during pregnancy. Estrogen has been shown to increase the production of the stress hormone cortisol, which raises the body's blood sugar and can lead to cravings for sugary foods. Progesterone is known to raise the body's metabolism and stimulate an appetite for all sorts of foods, including pickles.

But as we said, this is one of many explanations—and they're all inconclusive. Further proof, as if we needed any, that nerds in lab coats don't understand women.

Q If beans cause gas, why can't we use them to power our cars?

A There are two ways to consider this question.

Taking the high road, we can discuss the technology that transforms biomass into ethanol, a proven fuel for cars. Beans, like corn or virtually any other organic material, contain starches and complex carbohydrates that can be refined into ethanol, a combustible alcohol blended with gasoline to become that "green" E85 fuel you've heard about. Through fermentation—and with a lot of help from science—beans and their organic cousins can also find their way into methane gas, another proven biomass automotive fuel.

But how boring is the high road?

By "causing gas," this question really refers to the process by which the consumption of beans produces that bloated feeling that escapes us as . . . well . . . flatulence. High-fiber foods tend to cause intestinal gas, but beans seem to bear most of the blame, maybe because other world-class gas-promoters like cabbage

and Brussels sprouts aren't as big a part of our diet.

The culprit in these foods is a natural family of hard-to-digest sugars called oligosaccharides. These molecules boogie their way through our small intestine largely unmolested. The merrymaking begins when they hit the large intestine. Bacteria living there strap on the feedbag, chomping away at this nutritional bounty, multiplying even. Our intestinal gas is the by-product of their digestive action.

Most of this gas is composed of odorless hydrogen, nitrogen, and carbon dioxide. In some humans—about 30 percent of the adult population—this process also produces methane.

Ethanol isn't a part of the oligosaccharide equation. But hydrogen and methane are, and they're flammable gases. In fact, hydrogen is another player in the fuel-of-the-future derby and already powers experimental fuel-cell vehicles.

So order that chili and fill 'er up. Beans in your Beemer! Legumes for your Lexus!

No so fast, burrito boy. Setting aside the daunting biotechnical hurdle of actually capturing bean-bred flatulence from a person's, um, backside, the challenge becomes one of volume and storage.

Human flatulence simply doesn't contain hydrogen or methane in quantities sufficient to fuel anything more than a blue flame at a fraternity party. Even if we did generate enough of these gases to power a car, they'd have to be collected and carted around in high-pressure tanks to be effective as fuels.

Human biochemistry is a wonderful thing, but it isn't yet a backbone of the renewable-energy industry. For that, breathe a sigh of relief.

Q Does counting sheep help you fall asleep?

A The easiest way to work out the answer to this question is to try it out for yourself. Now, that's not an attempt to dodge the question—it turns out that opinions are divided about this issue. Some people say it works like a charm; others figure it doesn't work at all. The idea is that by counting sheep, you concentrate on something monotonous and boring, your brain slowly relaxes, and you fall asleep.

However, scientists at Oxford published a study in January 2002 claiming that counting sheep is less effective than imagining a waterfall or a beach. Their reason? Sheep are *too* boring. Counting them doesn't really use up any mental energy: It's simply an attempt to distract the brain from thinking about all those anxieties that everyone has late at night. Imagining a nice waterfall or beach calms the brain—the researchers found that the people in the study who imagined beaches or waterfalls fell asleep twenty minutes faster than those who counted sheep.

Researchers also found that it requires more mental energy to conjure up a detailed image. When counting sheep, some people will eventually find that they're just counting normally and not really imagining nice fluffy sheep leaping past their eyes.

In general, though, going to bed at the same time every day, increasing daily exercise, avoiding daytime naps, and cutting down on coffee or other products with caffeine should help you sleep easier. This way, you won't have to employ the services of a bunch of old sheep—they'd only stink up your bedroom anyway.

Q How do you know if you're colorblind?

A Most people say, "Red means stop and green means go." But suppose you say, "The top light means stop and the bottom means go." Or maybe your friend offers to meet you in a crowded place, saying, "Just look for the guy in the yellow pants and the red and green polka-dot shirt."; instead of making fun of his taste, you reply, "You'd better wear a hat so I'll be sure to see you."

If the words "red" and "green" mean nothing to you, you probably have a condition known as deuteranomaly, or red-green colorblindness. It's the most common form of colorblindness and affects 5 to 8 percent of the world's male population. Other, rarer, forms of color blindness include the inability to distinguish blue from yellow (trichromacy) and total monochromacy, the inability to perceive any color.

Colorblindness may seem weird to people with normal vision, but actually, we've all been there. All human infants are born colorblind. We only begin to see color around the age of four months when the retinas of our eyes are more developed.

How do we see color? The retina is composed of minute cells called rods and cones. The rods are most active in the dark, while the cones are most active in daylight. Because colors are most apparent in light, the cones are the main color receptors. We have three kinds of cones, and each absorbs one of three wavelengths of light: red, green, or blue. Scientists refer to this as trichromatic vision. The whole Crayola-box palette of colors our brains process comes from combining shades of red, yellow, and blue. It stands to reason, then, that any defect in one or more of the cones would affect our sense of color.

Colorblindness is considered a hereditary disorder. This is why fewer women are colorblind. A man, who has X and Y chromosomes, only needs to inherit a gene for color blindness from one parent, while a woman, with her pair of X chromosomes, would need to inherit the gene from both parents.

How do you know if you are colorblind? The most common detector is the Ishihara Test, which consists of a series of colored numbers written in small dots against a contrasting background of similar dots. If you have trouble reading one or more of the numbers, you may have impaired color perception.

In most cases, colorblindness is not a serious disability. In fact, if you are colorblind, you're in good company. Fred Rogers—yes, *the* Mister Rogers—was colorblind. And Emerson Moser, a senior production worker at Crayola for thirty-seven years, was also colorblind. His co-workers didn't know until he told them upon his retirement in 1990. And your friend in the yellow pants and red and green polka-dot shirt? Hmmm. Come to think of it, he might be just a bit colorblind, too.

Q Why do you shiver when you pee?

A Everything has a name. The notorious "pee shiver" is known by the impressive-sounding "post-micturition convulsion syndrome." "Micturition" is another word for urination, so it could read "after-pee shiver syndrome." It was thought for a long time that pee shivers were a largely male thing, but females experience it, too. As to why people experience it, that's a little tricky, since there hasn't been much research into the complexities of pee shivers.

There are a few theories, though. One of the most common is that when you urinate, all that warm urine—hopefully you weren't enjoying a meal while reading this—leaves your body at once, upsetting your body temperature and causing you to shiver. However, we don't experience the same thing while defecating.

Another theory is that we lose heat because we have to expose our nether regions to the elements. However, babies with nice warm diapers have been known to shiver while doing the deed.

A final theory has to do with the autonomic nervous system (ANS), which is what keeps your body conditions stable and constant. The ANS is split into the sympathetic nervous system (SNS) and the parasympathetic nervous system (PNS). The SNS generally relaxes the bladder and contracts the urethral sphincter, pretty much so that you don't pee in your pants. The PNS reverses that so you can relieve yourself. The more pressure in your bladder, the harder the SNS works to keep you from having an accident. It urges the brain to release catecholamine chemicals like dopamine, epinephrine, and norepinephrine. Catecholamines are chemicals that cause physiological changes to prepare the body for physical activity. When you finally get the chance to go to the toilet, the PNS takes over and rapidly changes the amount of catecholamines produced, perhaps causing the shiver. If this theory is true, the pee shiver should occur equally in men and women, but it tends to occur more in men.

So the jury is out on pee shivers. Hopefully some bright and brave young soul will dedicate his or her life to figuring it all out. Until then, keep it to yourself, especially over dinner.

Q Are noogies a cause of baldness?

A Your first reaction might be that this question is the comic relief—the clown we're sending in to make everyone laugh before we turn to harder, more serious topics. Well, what if we said, yes, noogies are a cause of baldness? That's right. And if you're the type who spent most of high school peering out through the metal slats of whichever locker you were thrust inside, you might want to pay attention.

First, a word about baldness: Baldness, or thinning hair, usually occurs for one of two reasons. Either your hair falls out at a faster rate than it can grow back or your hair follicles shrink to the point that they can no longer produce hair. Genetics are usually to blame for baldness, but certain medical treatments (such as chemotherapy) or diseases (lupus) can also cause your hair to fall out, either temporarily or permanently.

Where do noogies fit in? Don't get your pocket protector in a bunch; we're getting to it. Isn't it possible that one could receive a noogie so devastating—child behavioral therapists might even call it an "atomic noogie"—that it could damage the follicles, or even kill them? Eh, probably not. We'd be talking about a truly epic noogie. The noogie would either have to result in scarring (because new hair does not grow from scars), or it would have to be so powerful that it would damage the blood vessels that feed the follicles beneath the scalp. So while it's technically possible, the planet probably hasn't yet seen the knuckles that can deliver an atomic noogie.

Okay, what about stress? It is a well-documented fact that stress can lead to hair loss. Perhaps the fear associated with living under a *blitzkrieg* of noogies could cause the kind of stress that would result in hair loss. Or maybe a truly humiliating noogie could get the job done. Let's say you're in the middle of asking that girl you've had your eye on all year to the prom, only to have your invitation cut short by an unexpected headlock and searing noogie. Surely such a public emasculation could produce a type of post-traumatic noogie stress disorder that would cripple your hair production.

To be fair, it's speculative to claim that stress causes permanent baldness. Even if the noogie was so stressful that it caused hair loss, when the stress faded, your hair would grow normally again. And even if your hair didn't grow back, the culprit technically would be the stress, not the noogie. So, upon further review, noogies don't really cause baldness. Sorry—send in the clowns.

Q Can a person spontaneously combust?

A A photo documents the gruesome death of Helen Conway. Visible in the black-and-white image taken in 1964 in Delaware County, Pennsylvania, is an oily smear that was her torso and, behind, an ashen specter of the upholstered bedroom chair she occupied. The picture's most haunting feature might be her legs, thin and ghostly pale, clearly intact and seemingly unscathed by whatever it was that consumed the rest of her.

What consumed her, say proponents of a theory that people can catch fire without an external source of ignition, was spontaneous human combustion. It's a classic case, believers assert: Conway was immolated by an intense, precisely localized source of heat that damaged little else in the room. Adding to the mystery, the investigating fire marshal said that it took just twenty-one minutes for her to burn away and that he could not identify an outside accelerant.

If Conway's body ignited from within and burned so quickly she had no time to rise and seek help, hers wouldn't be the first or last death to fit the pattern of spontaneous human combustion.

The phenomenon was documented as early as 1763 by French-man Jonas Dupont in his collection of accounts, published as *De Incendis Corporis Humani Spontaneis*. Charles Dickens's

1852 novel *Bleak House* sensationalized the issue with the spontaneous-combustion death of a character named Krook. That humans have been reduced to ashes with little damage to their surroundings is not the stuff of fiction, however. Many documented cases exist. The question is, did these people combust spontaneously?

Theories advancing the concept abound. Early hypotheses held that victims, such as Dickens's Krook, were likely alcoholics so besotted that their very flesh became flammable. Later conjecture blamed the influence of geomagnetism. A 1996 book by John Heymer, *The Entrancing Flame,* maintained emotional distress could lead to explosions of defective mitochondria. These outbursts cause cellular releases of hydrogen and oxygen and trigger crematory reactions in the body. That same year, Larry E. Arnold—publicity material calls him a parascientist—published *Ablaze! The Mysterious Fires of Spontaneous Human Combustion.*

Arnold claimed sufferers were struck by a subatomic particle he had discovered and named the "pyrotron."

Perhaps somewhat more credible reasoning came out of Brooklyn, New York, where the eponymous founder of Robin Beach Engineers Associated (described as a scientific detective agency) linked the theory of spontaneous human combustion with proven instances of individuals whose biology caused them to retain intense concentrations of static electricity.

Skeptics are legion. They suspect that accounts are often embellished or important facts are ignored. That the unfortunate Helen Conway was overweight and a heavy smoker, for instance, likely played a key role in her demise.

Indeed, Conway's case is considered by some to be evidence of the wick effect, which might be today's most forensically respected explanation for spontaneous human combustion. It holds that an external source, such as a dropped cigarette, ignites bedding, clothing, or furnishings. This material acts like an absorbing wick, while the body's fat takes on the fueling role of candle wax. The burning fat liquefies, saturating the bedding, clothing, or furnishings, and keeps the heat localized.

The result is a long, slow immolation that burns away fatty tissues, organs, and associated bone, leaving leaner areas, such as legs, untouched. Experiments on pig carcasses show it can take five or more hours, with the body's water boiling off ahead of the spreading fire.

Under the wick theory, victims are likely to already be unconscious when the fire starts. They're in closed spaces with little moving air, so the flames are allowed to smolder, doing their work without disrupting the surroundings or alerting passersby.

Nevertheless, even the wick effect theory, like all other explanations of spontaneous human combustion, has scientific weaknesses. The fact remains, according to the mainstream science community, that evidence of spontaneous human combustion is entirely circumstantial, and that not a single proven eyewitness account exists to substantiate anyone's claims of "Poof—the body just went up in flames!"

Q Why does helium make your voice squeaky?

A Everyone loves balloons, especially the ones filled with helium. Wat's great about helium-filled balloons is not just the cheery way they float along, but also the way the gas inside alters your vocal cords. By inhaling small amounts of helium, a person can change his or her voice from its regular timbre to a squeaky, cartoonlike sound. But how does it work?

The simplest explanation is that since helium is six times less dense than air—the same reason a helium balloon floats—your vocal cords behave slightly differently when they're surrounded by helium. Additionally, the speed of sound is nearly three times faster in helium than in regular air, and that fact lends quite a bit of squeak to your voice as well.

The opposite reaction can be achieved using a chemical known as sulfur hexafluoride, though it's nowhere near as common as helium and much more expensive. Whereas helium is readily available in grocery and party stores, sulfur hexafluoride is generally used in electrical power equipment, meaning that one would have to order somewhat large quantities of it from a specially licensed provider. If you do manage to get hold of some, the results are plenty entertaining: Sulfur hexafluoride drops your voice incredibly low, much like that of a disc jockey or a super villain.

It's important to note, however, that inhaling helium (or other similar gases) is dangerous. There's a high risk of suffocating, because a person's lungs aren't designed to handle large quantities of helium. What's more, the canisters used to fill balloons contain more than just helium—there are other substances in there that help properly inflate a balloon that can be harmful to your body if they're inhaled. So while a helium-laced voice sounds funny, it actually shouldn't be taken as a joke.

Q What causes zits?

A   Contrary to popular belief, it doesn't matter if you're a pizza-loving preteen or a raw-food-obsessed forty-something—zits can strike anyone, at any age, at any time. The belief that tweens and teens are the only ones who get zits is the most widely held misconception about acne, the world's most common skin disorder. The good news is, there are clear answers to what causes zits, making these bothersome blemishes much easier to treat.

Zits have four major causes, and a possible fifth cause is hotly debated among dermatologists and allergists:

- Hormones
- Overactive oil glands
- Buildup of normal skin bacteria
- Irregular or excessive skin shedding of dead skin cells inside the pore and on the surface of the skin (common in teens)
- Reactions to cosmetics, specific foods, or medicines

Zits—whiteheads, papules, and pustules—form when dead skin cells mix with excess oil, also called sebum. This pugnacious cocktail plugs the pore, which causes a sometimes-painful swelling. Bacteria can also thrive in this mix, leading to infection and pus.

Some of the different factors that can cause hormones to increase oil production include puberty, stress, pregnancy, menstruation, birth control pills, corticosteroids, and lithium. It is believed that some people have a genetic predisposition that creates an overactive oil gland—or abnormal sebum—that produces oil that is too thick or irritating to the skin, or a malfunctioning pore lining that doesn't shed like normal pores.

Buildup of normal skin bacteria happens when oil is trapped in the hair follicles and *propionibacterium acnes* (*P. acnes*) grows in the blocked pore. The skin bacteria produce chemicals, which alter the composition of the oil, making the bacteria more irritating to the skin than usual. This causes inflammation, and a zit forms. It is unknown why some people experience a buildup of normal skin bacteria and some don't.

Although the fifth-mentioned cause for zits has been hotly debated, numerous studies suggest that oil-based cosmetics, medicines that contain iodides and bromides, and foods that contain gluten or dairy can cause a reaction (or zits) in certain allergic individuals.

To treat zits, there are a number of effective topical and oral medications available over the counter or by prescription, so talk with your dermatologist for more details. And for allergic individuals, allergists say that all you have to do is eliminate triggers and your zits will magically disappear. That's welcome news for self-conscious teenagers everywhere.

Q Why do men sometimes wake up with an erection for no particular reason?

A Referred to in the scientific community as "morning wood" or "morning glory," you probably recognize this phenomenon from its more colloquial name, "nocturnal penile tumescence." Whatever you choose to call it, morning erections are a normal part of male sexuality—so much so that studies of morning erections are used to determine whether a patient's erectile dysfunction stems from a psychological or physiological cause.

Relaxation is the key element here. While most people logically assume that the erectee is having an exciting dream about Pamela Anderson, or at least about finding a sports bar with a free buffet and drink specials, the cause of a shut-eye stiffie is completely neurochemical. Believe it or not, men can actually prevent themselves from getting an erection. The brain stem, also known as the primitive brain, sends signals to the spinal cord to decrease sexual responses and stop an erection before it starts. This is believed to be a response meant to protect men from inopportune erections, whether when running away from a saber-toothed tiger or simply going to the doctor for a physical.

However, during rapid eye movement (REM) sleep, the systems in the brain that prevent erections begin to shut down. As a result, men typically form several erections during a night's sleep, some of which last as long as two hours. These boners often are still there in the morning.

See? There's nothing sexual about it. Seriously, though, if you find that sweet sports bar, drop us a line.

Q What are boogers?

A Boogers are you. And be glad for it. If you're like most people, you regard those little crusty, slimy things with distaste and endeavor to remove them with haste. But before you turn up your nose—which admittedly does help in extracting the little, um, boogers—consider the following:

Boogers are made up largely of dried mucus, and your body produces mucus from head to toe, figuratively speaking. Your eyes, stomach, intestines, lungs, mouth, and urinary tract all produce mucus as a way of eliminating unhealthy materials from your body and of keeping unhealthy foreign materials from entering. Gross as mucus is, it actually helps keep you clean.

Boogers are a particularly unusual type of mucus. It's because of where that mucus appears: in the hairy little wind tunnels that are your nostrils. All day long your nose produces mucus—a quart of it, believe it or not. Most of this ends up back inside you, in your throat or belly. But a bit of it combines with dust and dirt and whatever else is whooshing up your nose, and ends up congealing to greater or lesser extent right on the spot. Boogers are largely harmless—although doctors recommend that you don't remove them with your fingers, because fingers contain germs and because a clumsy digit can do minor damage to the very mucous membranes that created the booger's main material.

Now, if you're scientifically inclined, you probably are wondering what mucus is, exactly. It's a "branched polysaccharide"—in other words, a sugar chain, like starch. Add a little water to starch and you get a sticky snotlike substance; let the water dry up and the whole thing hardens. Hey, you can simulate the whole booger-making process right at your kitchen table! Or you can just take the word of the late comic George Carlin: "Snot: the original rubber cement."

Q Do people still mummify corpses?

A The ancient Egyptians would be happy to know that five thousand years later, mummification is still around. The processes have changed, but if you want your corpse preserved like King Tut's was, you have options. In fact, you could even end up on the museum circuit, just like the boy king.

Mummification simply means keeping some soft tissue—such as skin or muscle—around long after death. To make a mummy, you just need to keep the tissue from being eaten. Shooing vultures and cannibals away is simple enough, but keeping hungry bacteria at bay is no small feat. The trick is to make the body inhospitable to bacteria. Bacteria like it hot and wet, so mummification depends on keeping a body extremely cold and/or dry.

The ancient Egyptians removed the corpse's internal organs, filled the cavity with linen pads, sprinkled the body with a drying compound called natron, and then wrapped it in bandages. In 1994, Egyptology professor Bob Brier successfully replicated this process—but most other modern mummy-makers use other means.

When Vladimir Lenin croaked in 1924, the Russians decided to mummify him. Their secret process involved immersing the corpse in a chemical bath that replaces all water. The results are impressive—Lenin today looks like Lenin on his deathbed. In 1952, the Argentineans took a similar tack with Eva Peron, the wife of dictator Juan Peron. They replaced bodily fluids with wax, making a wax dummy corpse.

Since 1967, dozens of people have opted for cryonics, a form of mummification in which doctors replace the water in the body with chemicals, and keep the deceased at a crisp -320 degrees Fahrenheit—at least until scientists figure out how to cure death.

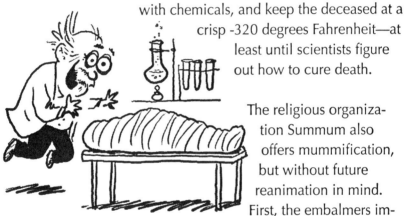

The religious organization Summum also offers mummification, but without future reanimation in mind. First, the embalmers immerse the body in a chemical solution for thirty to sixty days to dissolve the water in the body. Next, they wrap the body in gauze and apply a layer of polyurethane, followed by a layer of fiberglass and resin. The body is then sealed in a bronze or stainless steel mummiform capsule. Summun has a growing list of (still-living) human clients. The organization asks for a donation to cover its services, usually $67,000 for the process—not including the mummiform.

The most impressive modern mummies come from a process called Plastination. First, embalmers pump a substance that halts decay into the corpse. Then, they remove the skin and other tissues, and immerse the body in an acetone solution, which dissolves the water and fats. Next, they immerse the body in liquid plastic inside a vacuum chamber and drop the pressure until the acetone boils and evaporates. The resulting vacuum in the body sucks in the plastic so that it permeates every nook and cranny. Before the liquid solidifies into hard plastic, embalmers pose the body. The result is a clean, educational sculpture, which also happens to be an actual corpse.

German anatomist Gunther von Hagens invented Plastination in 1977, and he's signed up nearly eight thousand body donors— many of whom are now mummies in the traveling Body Worlds exhibition. The good news is that it's completely free to join its ranks. To sign up, contact the Institute for Plastination (bodydonation@plastination.com), review all the gory details, then sign a statement of intent, a stack of consent forms, and a body donor ID card. If you're looking to stick around after you pass on and don't mind posing with tourists for the next few thousand years, the value is hard to beat.

Q Can you actually get scared to death?

A Scientists say you can. It's not the fear itself that kills you, but the physical reactions that fear provokes. There seem to be two broad types of "death from fear": the kind brought on by a sudden fright and the kind that's provoked by a general sense of dread.

What the heck, let's take the slow version first. A study published in the *British Medical Journal* in 2002 noted that Chinese and

Japanese people living in the United States are 13 percent more likely to die on the fourth day of the month than on any other day. This was determined after analyzing 209,908 death certificates of Chinese and Japanese people in America and comparing them with 47,000 Caucasians' death certificates, considering cause of death, inpatient status, age, sex, and marital status for each.

The likely cause of the increase? The dread throughout much of the Asian world of the number four, which is linguistically similar to the word for "death" in Mandarin, Cantonese, and Japanese. It is frightful in the way the number thirteen is in some Western societies—perhaps even more so.

"It is not an all-or-none phenomenon, but the perception of bad luck, a good holiday, or a birthday may shift the odds of dying at that particular time," Stanford psychiatrist David Spiegel, M.D., told *Psychiatric News*, commenting on the study, which was conducted by University of California at San Diego sociologist David P. Phillips, Ph.D. In other words, fear can cause stress that makes the body more vulnerable to death at that time.

This is played out in a more dramatic fashion in sudden death from fear—from fright or shock, to be more accurate. Neurologist Martin A. Samuels, of Brigham and Women's Hospital in Boston, studied hundreds of cases of sudden death and found that catastrophic or intensely frightening events can cause the heart to stop, due to its inability to handle chemicals that the brain sends out during times of great stress.

"We all carry this little bomb inside us," Samuels told ABC News. "It would be like getting an enormous dose of [the drugs] speed or ecstasy." He added, "I know this because I have cases of children with absolutely no heart disease who died on amusement park rides."

And you thought the Fun House was scary.

Q Does a bigger brain make you smarter?

A If you're someone who has an oversized noggin—and displays it like a trophy—we really hate to rain on your parade. But we're going to anyway: You are not smarter than the rest of us. Scientific studies continue to show that size isn't everything where the human brain is concerned.

Sure, it might be easy to assume that a colossal cranium is capable of holding more intelligence—just by sheer mass. History suggests otherwise. William H. Calvin, a theoretical neurophysiologist and affiliate professor emeritus at the University of Washington School of Medicine, points to notable periods in the historical timeline when the brain mass of ancient humans greatly increased, but toolmaking smarts did not. Although *Homo sapiens* in Africa two hundred thousand years ago had developed a brain size comparable to that of contemporary people, they continued to use the same crude, round-edged rocks for some one hundred and fifty thousand years before graduating to points, needles, harpoons, and hooks. You can't exactly say those bigger-brained primates were the sharpest tools in the shed.

As for modern people, advancements in magnetic resonance imaging (MRI)-based brain scans are giving researchers more pertinent data about the relationship between brain size and intelligence. (Before MRI, researchers had to measure the outside of a person's head to estimate brain size, or wait until that person died to get an accurate measurement.) A 2004 study conducted by researchers at the University of California-Irvine and the University of New Mexico was one of the first to use MRI technology to demonstrate that it's not overall brain size that counts, but brain organization.

How so? The researchers used MRI to get structural scans of the study participants' brains, and then compared those scans to respective scores on standard IQ tests. What they discovered was that human intelligence is less about total girth and more about the volume and specific location of gray-matter tissue across the brain. It appears there are several "smart" areas of the brain related to IQ, and having more gray matter in those locations is one of the things that makes us, well, smarter.

Undoubtedly, the relationship between brain size and intelligence will continue to be studied and debated, but some in the medical field now believe that brain size is purely a function of genetics and doesn't result in a greater intellect. Researchers at Harvard Medical School have even been able to identify two of the genes (beta-catenin and ASPM) that regulate brain size.

So if you've got a big head, don't be so quick to get a big head. It turns out that Albert Einstein's brain weighed only 2.7 pounds. That's 10 percent smaller than average.

Q Why do your ears pop in an airplane?

A Frequent air travelers know they can rely on a few things during each flight. One, a minibag of pretzels and a plastic cup of warm Sprite will be the poor excuse for an in-flight meal. Two, the in-flight entertainment will be a Jim Carrey movie, most likely *Ace Ventura II*. And three, twenty minutes before landing, the infant who has been sleeping peacefully in the row behind you will wake up and begin shrieking nonstop until you land. Is *Ace Ventura II* that bad? Well, yes, it is. But that's probably not why the child is shrieking. More likely, it's because of excruciating ear pain.

Right behind your eardrum is something called the middle ear, a little air-filled space that helps in the transmission of acoustic waves. The air pressure in the middle ear is imperative to your tympanic health—too much pressure and the eardrum could burst; too little and it could collapse. Usually, that air pressure is pretty stable because of how air pressure works in the environment. As we remember from physics class (okay, as we nerds remember from physics class), air pressure changes with altitude—the higher you get, the lower the pressure.

Whenever air pressure changes, the air pressure in the middle ear also must change to reach equilibrium with the external air pressure. When you're rising—such as during takeoff—the pressure in your middle ear is greater than the pressure outside, and air needs to escape. The escape hatch is known as the Eustachian tube, which connects the middle ear to the throat. During takeoff, this pressure calibration is pretty easy for your ear to achieve on its own. (Think of how easy it is for an inflated balloon to release air.)

However, landing is another story. As a plane descends, the pressure outside becomes greater than the pressure in your middle ear. Left untended, that pressure difference can create a vacuum that makes for a pretty painful earache. Fortunately, we grown-ups know how to force open the Eustachian tube, allowing air to rush into the middle ear and equal the pressure. This can be accomplished by swallowing, chewing gum, blowing your nose, or yawning. The popping you hear during takeoff and landing is the sound of the air rushing in or out of your middle ear.

This also explains why babies tend to shriek on airplanes. Because infants are not capable of willfully forcing open their Eustachian tubes, they simply suffer as the air pressure outside begins to change. One solution is to give the baby a pacifier or bottle, as the sucking motion can help unblock the Eustachian tube and relieve some of that middle-ear pain. If this doesn't work, try turning off the in-flight entertainment.

Q Why do you always wake up just before you die in a dream?

A The answer to this question is obvious if you've seen Wes Craven's *A Nightmare on Elm Street*. Remember the main character, Freddy Krueger? Bad acne, needed a manicure—yeah, that guy. As Freddy (or more accurately, his victims) taught us, if you die in your dreams, you die in real life. There's your answer. Next question, please.

Wait, what's that? Craven isn't an authority on dream psychology? Movies aren't real?

Sorry to disappoint. Millions of children were frightened out of their pajamas by Freddy Krueger in the 1980s, but one of the underlying premises of the film and its seemingly endless stream of sequels—that dying in dream reality causes death in waking reality—has zero basis in fact. Still, the myth Craven tapped into has persisted for a long time. One of the reasons is that for many people, the dream world is as terrifying—and about as well understood—as death itself. And it follows a certain logic: After all, other dreams can affect our physical self, such as...well, you know what kind.

Another reason for the myth is that most people don't die in their dreams. Oh, they get close. But most people, whether they're plunging from the fiftieth story of a building or about to be hacked apart by fingernail blades, wake up just before the moment of truth. In fact, the dream of falling to certain death only to wake up just before impact is so common that it appears in just about every dream-analysis manual out there.

Dream experts have been baffled by this phenomenon. Though they haven't come up with a definitive explanation, some theorists believe it may have to do with myoclonic jerks. No, not your idiot neighbors who crank Metallica at three in the morning—myoclonic jerks are involuntary spasms of the muscles that jolt you out of sleep. These jerks most often strike just as you're drifting off to sleep (usually accompanied by a falling sensation), but they can also occur during rapid eye movement (REM) states.

Like many sleep and dream phenomena, researchers aren't sure what causes myoclonic jerks. One theory holds that as your body drifts into sleep, the brain mistakes the total relaxation of the muscles as a loss of bodily control. In a desperate but misguided attempt to regain control, the brain rouses the body into a conscious, hyperalert state. As we know from our pubescence, the body can't always tell the difference between dreams and reality, so it would hold that an intense dream, especially one that involves death, might induce one of these myoclonic jerks, waking you up just in the nick of time.

The death-by-dreaming myth unravels even more with a cursory glance through the annals of dream research. Numerous subjects have reported dying in dreams and waking up the next day to tell about it. So all of those folks who have been terrified by *A Nightmare on Elm Street* don't need to fret about Freddy Krueger invading their dreams. It's those people under the stairs they should be worried about.

Chapter Five

FOOD AND DRINK

Q Can coffee kill you?

A Sure, if you drink a keg of it. Scientists with too much time on their hands have postulated that you would need to drink between eighty and one hundred cups of coffee—one even says it's more like two hundred cups—in rapid succession before the caffeine somehow fried your system.

Now, it's possible the number is lower than the experts claim. A young woman spent a day in the hospital after drinking seven double espressos at her parents' sandwich shop and experiencing uncontrolled sobbing, serious heart palpitations, breathing problems, and a fever, according to news reports. Could working for your folks really be that painful? Regardless, you'd have to ingest a prodigious—and absurd—amount of coffee before it could kill you.

On the other hand, some coffee each day is good for you in about a million different ways, scientists are now telling us. Curiously, many of the benefits seem greatest in those who are heavy coffee drinkers—and the risks, such as they are, tend to be greater for those who are very light drinkers. For instance, studies have shown a higher risk of heart attack in those who don't regularly drink coffee. For them, even one cup can be harmful, apparently because the caffeine is more of a shock to their system. A researcher said that one cup of coffee for a non-regular coffee drinker could be "the final straw," but one suspects that something else would have felled those subjects anyway, if not a cup of joe.

What are coffee's health benefits? Here's what some studies say:

Coffee might lessen the risk of type 2 diabetes, especially in people who drink more than six cups a day. The risk in such men goes down by more than 50 percent. (However, if you have type 2 diabetes, drinking coffee can put your blood sugar level out of whack.)

Coffee can lower the risk of Parkinson's disease, especially when consumed liberally. Two cups a day can lower the risk of colon cancer by 25 percent and of gallstones by 40 percent or more. Four or more cups a day can lower the risk of cirrhosis of the liver by 80 percent.

Coffee seems to help manage asthma and help control attacks when they happen. It might stop headaches, prevent cavities, and boost athletic performance (more by sharpening the mind than the body). Not a single study has shown that coffee is harmful to kids, and one study suggests that drinking coffee with milk can help kids avoid depression. Nevertheless, the National Institute of Health cautions that caffeine intake by children needs to be carefully monitored.

So, coffee is not for everyone. There are fast and slow caffeine metabolizers—this seems to be genetically determined—and if you're one of the latter, the caffeine hangs out in your body longer and makes you especially susceptible to a kind of nervousness. Coffee blocks certain tension-controlling hormones, so you may be more likely to have a nonfatal heart attack if you drink a couple cups a day. Coffee also has been shown to raise blood pressure slightly and temporarily—but not permanently.

It's common wisdom that every medicine has its benefits and risks, and coffee—though not a controlled substance, thank God—is no different. Despite the occasional scary scientific study (some of which are quickly contradicted) and being a proven risk to those whose tickers are finicky to begin with, coffee seems just a few sips short of a miracle drug. Is that your foot that's tapping nonstop, or mine?

Q How sweet are sweetbreads?

A A tip for those who rarely eat at trendy restaurants: If you see sweetbreads on the menu, don't start salivating at the thought of a warm muffin with butter dripping down the sides.

Instead, picture the thymus gland or pancreas of a young sheep, cow, or pig. Then exhale deeply and start focusing on taking a swig or two from your glass of wine.

Sweetbreads are a delicacy enjoyed throughout the world by people with adventurous palates, but the burger-and-fries types might not understand such culinary wanderlust. In fact, they might want to ask the question: What in the name of the Golden Arches is a thymus gland? The answer isn't pretty. A thymus gland contains two lobes, one in the throat and the other near the heart. The lobe near the heart—particularly from milk-fed young calves—is considered the best to eat because of its smooth texture and mild taste; as a result, it will cost you more at that trendy restaurant. Pancreas sweetbreads, or stomach sweetbreads, are much less common than their thymus counterparts.

Sweetbreads and other edible internal organs are often grouped together using the term "offal" (which, for those still ready to vomit, isn't a word for "awful" in some foreign language). It means the "off-fall," or the off-cuts, of a carcass.

Since sweetbreads aren't sweet and aren't bread, how did they get their name? This is something of a mystery. The *historie of man*, published in 1578, sheds a splash of light on the matter: "A certaine Glandulous part, called Thimus, which in Calues … is most pleasaunt to be eaten. I suppose we call it the sweete bread." Translation: They tasted good.

Back in those roughhewn days—before butcher shops and grocery stores—sweetbreads weren't considered a delicacy. Families butchered their own livestock and often ate every part, including the thymus gland and pancreas. Today, sweetbreads are prepared in many ways: You can poach, roast, sear, braise, or sauté 'em, and often season them with salt, pepper, onions, garlic, or thyme.

If you want to prepare sweetbreads, we have two pieces of advice. First, sweetbreads are extremely perishable, so be sure to cook them within twenty-four hours of your purchase. Second, they're probably not the ideal dish to serve on a first date.

Q How cool are cucumbers?

A In his poem "A New Song of New Similes," eighteenth-century English author John Gay wrote, "I'd be...cool as a cucumber could see the rest of womankind." Not at all unwittingly, Gay coined a phrase that has become part of our collective consciousness. But are cucumbers really all that cool?

Let's turn back the clock a few hundred years. Imagine you're in India, the supposed birthplace of the cucumber. It's about one hundred degrees in the shade. You've just polished off a dish of delectable but fiery hot vindaloo chicken, and now it feels like steam is shooting out of your ears and nostrils, like you're a character in a Warner Brothers cartoon. Instinctively, you reach for a glass of ice water. But wait. In your dizzy, sweaty haste, you've forgotten that refrigeration—and Warner Brothers cartoons, for that matter—won't be invented for centuries.

There is no ice water! How do you extinguish the fire that rages in your mouth? That's right: You reach for a few slices of cool cucumber, and they really hit the spot.

While there's no reason to believe that its physical temperature is lower than that of any other vegetable, the cucumber's mild flavor and watery flesh give it a refreshing quality that has made it a favorite warm-weather ingredient in cooling salads, relishes, and yogurt sauces for generations. It should come as no surprise that the cucumber hails from the same family of plants (*Cucurbiticeae*) as the watermelon.

But there is evidence to suggest that cucumbers can keep you "cool" in other ways. The cucumber's skin is a source of fiber, and several studies have shown that a high-fiber diet may help to lower your blood pressure, a benefit for those who share some of the personality traits of certain steam-shooting cartoon characters. And when applied directly to the skin, the ascorbic acid (vitamin C) and caffeic acid found in the cucumber can help soothe and seemingly cool irritations and reduce swelling.

You may have heard of another, nondietary use for cucumbers. Rock stars have been known to stuff them into their pants to enhance a certain physical feature. The "prop" couldn't be sillier, but they think it makes them look cool.

Q Is it possible to eat just one potato chip?

A Since 1963, potato chip–maker Lay's has been taunting us with the slogan "Betcha can't eat just one." And we all know a binge session of salty-crunchy-greasy goodness is pretty tough to avoid. In Lay's TV ads, even the likes of Cal Ripken, Jr. (the "iron man" of baseball) failed the challenge. Could eating just one potato chip be the ultimate test of a person's will? Well, in case you haven't heard, where there's a will, there's a way.

Let's say, for instance, you could get your mouth around one potato chip that just happened to be super-colossal in size. At the Idaho Potato Expo in Blackfoot, Idaho, you'll find a single crisp that measures twenty-five by fourteen inches. Made by the Proctor and Gamble Company in Jackson, Tennessee, in 1991, this Pringles chip holds a spot in the *Guinness Book of World Records* as "the world's largest potato crisp." It weighs 5.4 ounces and contains 920 calories. You'd have to munch down eighty normal Pringles' chips to reach that same number of calories.

This VIP (Very Important Pringle) is encased in glass, so it might be tricky to get your hands on it. A *Mission: Impossible*–style break-in might be worth it (you know, just to prove your point), but you can also demonstrate your "one chip" resolve at home. The best way to do this? First, rid your pantry of zesty taste-bud-traps like "salt & vinegar," "sweet BBQ," or "sour cream & onion" chips. These euphoria-inducing flavors only serve to beckon you to eat every last chip—and lick the inside of the empty bag, too.

To truly accomplish the one-chip-only feat, you've got to think outside the greasy, glimmering foil. That means trading in your beloved "salt & pepper" kettle chips for newfangled flavors that are a little more unsettling to the stomach. How about potato crisps seasoned with the essence of Atlantic lobster, chocolate marshmallow, or fried chicken skin?

Still can't stop eating 'em? Then some Asian-inspired "delights" might be your last hope. Care for a bowl of potato chips flavored with slimy seaweed or crispy squid? The latter (by Sepasang

Naga) was named "number 1 worst chip ever" by Taquitos.net, a snack food review site on the Web. Imagine popping open a fresh bag of chips to be greeted by the seaside aromas of "a three-day-old fish market in a third world" (according to Taquitos.net). We dare you to eat just one!

Q What is the tastiest part of the human body for cannibals?

A This question gets asked all the time. After all, what if the plane carrying your national rugby team crashes in the mountains, as happened to the Uruguayan team in 1972? Or your wagon train is trapped for the winter on a desolate mountain pass, like the infamous Donner Party? You may need to know just which cuts of human flesh are the tastiest in such situations.

Unfortunately, *Bon Appétit* has yet to publish its "Cannibal" issue—the headline will be easy to write: EAT ME! So we're forced to go to primary sources to determine which parts of the human body are the most succulent. Fortunately, there aren't many of them.

According to archaeological evidence, human cannibalism has a long history that dates back to the Neanderthals. Despite the stereotype that cannibals only live on remote islands, or in the deepest jungles, evidence of cannibalism has been found in cultures on nearly every continent, including Europe and North America. However, most cannibalistic practices throughout history were of a ritual nature, and there were few food critics writing up snappy reviews of their human feasts. For that, we have to consult those individuals throughout history who dined on other humans for pleasure.

The current living expert on cannibalism—Armin Meiwes, the German cannibal who is serving a life sentence for devouring a willing victim—likened the taste of his "cannibalee" to pork. Meiwes prepared his meal in a green pepper sauce, with a side of croquettes and Brussels sprouts. Science seems to agree with Meiwes. Some Japanese researchers manufactured "an electro-mechanical sommelier," a kind of gastronomist robot capable of sampling wines, cheeses, meats, and hors d'oeuvres, and identifying what it has been fed. When one reporter stuck his hand in the robot's maw, the two-foot robot immediately identified it as prosciutto. When the accompanying cameraman offered his hand, the mechanical gourmand declared, "Bacon."

So, what is the tastiest part of the human body? That seems to be a matter of debate. Early twentieth-century murderer and cannibal Albert Fish declared that the buttocks were the choicest cut, but latter-day cannibal Sagawa Issei disagrees, claiming that the thighs get that honor. In Fiji, where cannibalism was practiced until the late 1860s, men (women apparently were forbidden from partaking in this tasty treat) also favored the thighs (they also preferred the flesh of nonwhite women).

So if you really must know, there you have it: The thighs and buttocks are the prime cuts of a human. Just don't invite us to dinner.

Q Why doesn't broccoli come in a can?

A Broccoli is usually purchased in one of these ways: from the grocer's produce department or frozen-vegetable section, the farmer's market, or freeze-dried from any number of health-food stores or online merchants. If broccoli does happen to show up in a can, it's usually in the form of the tiny, mushy bits that float around in cream of broccoli soup.

Broccoli typically does not come in a can because the process used to pressure-can vegetables consists of boiling the vegetables at temperatures exceeding two hundred degrees Fahrenheit, draining them, placing them in hot jars, and covering them with boiling water again. This process softens the broccoli to the point of turning it into mush.

Another reason broccoli does not come in a can has less to do with health (broccoli actually retains the majority of its minerals, protein, and fatty acids during the canning process) and more to do with the intensity of the taste and smell of canned broccoli, which can be offensive to some. According to the *USDA Complete Guide to Home Canning*, broccoli is not recommended for canning because the processing intensifies strong flavors and discolors the rich green vegetable. The USDA suggests instead that you freeze broccoli to preserve or store it.

To prepare broccoli for freezing, blanch it in boiling water for three minutes or steam it for five minutes. Allow it to cool, then drain and package the vegetable, and put it in your freezer. It's a little more work, but at least the taste and smell won't scare away your houseguests.

Q Is the tomato a fruit or a vegetable?

A Botanically speaking, there's no question about it: The tomato is definitely a fruit. But before you say, "Whoa! How did a fruit get in my vegetable juice?" let's understand what a fruit really is.

By definition, a true fruit is the fleshy or dry ripened ovary of a plant flower that also contains the seeds of the plant. So that means oranges, grapes, and bananas are fruits, right? But what about other seeded foods like cucumbers, eggplants, squash, bean pods, almonds, corn kernels, and...tomatoes? Guess what? They're all fruits, too.

In broad terms, the botanical (and scientific) definition of fruit encompasses almost anything that contains seeds. So what are vegetables? Well, they're all the seedless crops that are left over— you know, the stuff your mom forced you to eat if you wanted pie for dessert. These include root crops like carrots and turnips, stems like asparagus, leaves like lettuce and cabbage, and flower buds like broccoli and cauliflower.

Why all the confusion? Some of the blame can be placed square- ly on the shoulders of the United States Supreme Court, whose 1893 case *Nix* v. *Hedden* dealt with whether the tomato should be classified as a fruit or a vegetable. Why would the Supreme Court possibly have given a hoot whether the tomato is a fruit or vegetable? It came down to money, of course. The issue related to the Tariff Act of 1883, which stipulated that there would be a 10 percent tax on imported vegetables but no tax on imported fruits.

The Supreme Court rejected the definition of the tomato as a monstrous botanical berry, instead deferring to its common culinary use. Justice Horace Gray stated: "Botanically speaking, tomatoes are the fruit of a vine, just as are cucumbers, squashes, beans, and peas. But in the common language of the people, whether sellers or consumers of provisions, all these are vegetables which are grown in kitchen gardens, and which, whether eaten cooked or raw, are, like potatoes, carrots, parsnips, turnips, beets, cauliflower, cabbage, celery, and lettuce, usually served at dinner in, with, or after the soup, fish, or meats which constitute the principal part of the repast, and not, like fruits generally, as dessert."

As the Supreme Court ruling pointed out, tomatoes are primarily eaten in the manner of a vegetable while fruits are usually used in desserts. That's pretty relatable. As far as cooking is concerned, we often associate natural plants that are savory to be vegetables and plants that are sweet to be fruits.

Now you know that's not correct—at least in a scientific sense. So tell your grocer, tell your friends, and tell the people who make tomato-based V8 and dare to call it "100 percent vegetable juice."

Q What makes honey so harmful to infants?

A Ah, sweet ambrosia of the queen bee! Sugar cane and maple sap aside, honey is perhaps the closest Mother Nature has come to manufacturing candy outright. It's gooey, sticky, and sweet, and it's the only way some people can stomach a cup of tea. Bears love it; in fact, a certain tubby yellow cubby is notorious for the lengths he will go for a "pawful" of the stuff. Rolling around in the mud, pretending to be a little black rain cloud, mooching off his friends: His addiction shows just how tasty honey can be.

But while honey is tasty, it can be very bad for your baby. The sweet stuff is somewhat of a Trojan horse, carrying entire battalions of harmful bacterial spores entrenched within its sticky goodness. These spores produce *Clostridium botulinum* bacteria. Once inside an infant, the bacteria set to work producing a toxin that can lead to infant botulism.

The Centers for Disease Control and Prevention (CDC) is not yet convinced of honey's role in infant botulism, a disease that has also been blamed for Sudden Infant Death Syndrome, or SIDS. There is not enough strong data to warrant a blanket warning regarding honey; however, the CDC hopes parents will look at the evidence for themselves and exercise caution when choosing which foods to give their babies. In the United Kingdom, every jar of honey sold bears a label advising parents against giving it to infants; it's been this way since the connection was made between honey and infant botulism in 1978. Why the CDC has not followed suit in the United States, one can only speculate.

Once a child reaches the twelve-month mark, pediatricians agree it is safe to include honey in your young one's diet. Not only that, but it's healthy and wholesome. Plus, as stated above, it's absolutely delicious. But as far as your baby is concerned, it's best to err on the side of caution.

DON'T FEED THE BEARS? Nay. DON'T FEED THE INFANTS!

Q Why does gin taste like pine needles?

A Simply put, it's the juniper berry that gives gin its piney fresh flavor. The taste of gin can be traced to this fleshy, scaly, and bitter seed cone, which comes from a shrub that, like the pine tree, is a member of the evergreen family.

The forerunner of gin, a Dutch spirit called *genever*, is said to have originated in Holland sometime in the early seventeenth century as a medicine for stomach ailments. Juniper berries flavored the concoction, and also lent their diuretic and anti-inflammatory qualities to the brew. The British soon stole the idea and began distilling their own version, called gin, which had certain...recreational benefits. Suffice it to say, by the mid-seventeen hundreds, more gin was consumed in England than beer.

Gin's popularity continued to grow, and sometime after the advent of the continuous still in 1831, the English began producing their own distinctive variety: London dry. Today, most of the gin produced around the world falls into the dry category. Dry gin begins with a more neutral base spirit rather than the sugary, malty one first used by the Dutch, so the botanical flavors that are added for the second phase of distilling come through more clearly. Juniper berries remain the most dominant flavoring, but manufacturers have developed formulas that include various combinations and proportions of other herbs and spices, such as angelica root, anise, coriander, caraway, lime, lemon and orange peels, licorice, cardamom, cassia, and grains of paradise.

Of course, where would gin be without tonic? The gin and tonic was born in the English colonies of India and Southeast Asia in the eighteen hundreds. Malaria was a scourge at the time, and quinine, a bitter tonic, was the treatment of choice. The problem was that quinine tasted like doodoo. To help the medicine go down, a little gin was mixed in. It proved to be quite tasty, and the rest is cocktail history.

Today, any number of other cocktails use gin, from the fruity Singapore Sling to the ever-popular dry martini. And to think, all this sprung from a little old juniper berry.

Q What exactly is in Spam?

A While your IT guy might tell you spam is an offensive unsolicited email, the original Spam was a packaged pork luncheon meat created by Jay Hormel in 1937. Nearly seven billion cans of Spam have been sold, and each year legions of fans congregate at festivals like Spamarama and Spam Jam to celebrate its meaty, salty goodness.

What is it that makes Spam, well, Spam? For starters, there's the distinctive vacuum-sealed tin. Hormel Foods Corporation says as long as no air gets into the can, Spam has a shelf-life of... forever. "It's like meat with a pause button," they exalt.

To that, one can only say, "Where's the remote?" After all, flavors like Hot & Spicy, Hickory Smoke, and Golden Honey Grail (a salty-sweet Spam created in honor of the Broadway musical Monty Python's Spamalot) are pretty hard to resist. Especially when you consider how boring regular old ham is in comparison.

Ham is from the upper part of a pig leg that's been salted and dried, or smoked. Spam, on the other hand, is a combination of ham and pork (pork being cuts from the pig shoulder or else-where). Add to that sugar, salt, water, a little potato starch, and a dash of sodium nitrate (for "pinkification" coloration), and you've got yourself a true meat marvel.

The history of Spam is almost as colorful as the meat itself. Spam was shipped overseas during World War II and fed to the Allied soldiers. Some over-the-top Spamheads go so far as to say the economical pork loaf helped the Allies achieve victory.

Today, Spam truly is a world power. It is made in factories all over the globe, from Austin, Minnesota; and Fremont, Nebraska; to Denmark, South Korea, and the Philippines. About ninety million cans of the stuff are sold each year.

As to how the luncheon meat got its name, some speculate it came from combining the words "spiced" and "ham." However, Hormel Foods says Jay Hormel held a contest to find a name. New York radio actor Kenneth Daigneau was crowned the win-ner, and for that he won a prize of one hundred dollars. What? No lifetime supply of Spam?

Q Why do chefs wear those ridiculous hats?

A As anybody who has ever worked in a restaurant can attest, the chef is the supreme dictator of the kitchen. Sometimes brilliant, often tempestuous, the chef rules the back of the house through a combination of respect and fear. Still, how can someone wearing such a ridiculous hat be taken seriously?

Outside of the pope, chefs may have the silliest headgear in the professional world. It's called a *toque blanche*, and it is a white, heavily starched embarrassment whose look ranges from a tall tube to an enormous, deformed mushroom.

Just how it came to be the symbol of chefdom is a matter of debate. Indeed, there are several theories about the origin of the chef's toque, none of which is substantiated with enough evidence to be confirmed as a sole explanation. One of these is that Henry VIII, outraged at finding a hair in his soup, ordered the beheading of his chef. Future chefs took note, making sure to cover their heads in order to save them.

A second theory holds that the chef's toque originated in ancient Assyria, long before the birth of Christ. Back then, poisoning was the favored method of assassination (hence, the dangerous profession of the royal food taster). Obviously, a chef was under scrutiny because he had the power to poison food. Proof of the chef's allegiance to his royal master was a "crown" he fashioned—a tall hat, made of cloth, that mimicked the actual crown worn by the king himself.

A third theory, and perhaps the most compelling, is that the toque originated in the sixth century AD, in the beginning of the Middle Ages. In those dark days, artists and intellectuals—groups that included chefs—were persecuted, and it was said that some of these luminaries protected themselves by taking shelter in monasteries. To disguise themselves, they donned the wardrobe of the clergy, which apparently included silly hats.

Though the earliest origins of the toque are debatable, it is known that the headwear evolved into its current form in France, the birthplace of *haute cuisine*. By the nineteenth century, forms of the toque were worn all over Europe, though their shapes varied.

In the late nineteenth century, the legendary French chef Auguste Escoffier brought order to the chaos and came up with a standard toque. Unfortunately, he decided that the tall, starched version of the chef's hat was ideal. In a way, it's not entirely surprising that the toque would find its ultimate form in France. It is the country, after all, that gave us another of the all-time silliest hats: the beret.

Q What does humble pie taste like?

A Which would you rather swallow: your pride or a mouthful of deer gizzard? Actually, original recipes for humble pie included the heart, liver, and other internal organs of a deer, or even a cow or boar. Talk about your awful offal!

The term "humble pie" derives from "umble pie," which dates back roughly to fourteenth-century England. The term "numbles," then later "umbles," referred to those aforementioned, um, select bits of a deer carcass. Umble pie was eaten by servants, whose lords feasted on the more palatable cuts of venison or whatever beast was being served. If meat was on the menu and you were eating umble pie, you were likely to be in a lower or more inferior position in society. The transition from the original term to the pun "humble pie" was an easy one, given that some English dialects silence the "h" at the beginning of a word.

For some unfathomable reason, modern-day recipes for humble pie do exist, although these call, mercifully, for cuts of beef or other meat. Others are more customary dessert pies with sweet fillings that inspire humility only when you're in the presence of a bathroom scale.

So the next time you've done somebody wrong, just apologize, take your lumps, wait for time to heal the wound, and consider yourself fortunate. It's better to spend "thirty days in the hole," to quote the 1970s British supergroup Humble Pie, than to eat a boar's intestines.

Q Is there a real Aunt Jemima?

A No, there has never been a real Aunt Jemima. Every part of her persona, from her look to her legendary baking prowess, was dreamed up by a couple of guys in suits—Chris L. Rutt and Charles G. Underwood, inventors of the first instant pancake mix and owners of the Pearl Milling Company.

Both the name and the image were inspired by a minstrel show that Rutt attended in 1889. The actors in the show performed a song called "Old Aunt Jemima" in blackface, aprons, and bandannas. And just like that, an icon was born.

The mascot couldn't keep the company afloat, though, and the Pearl Milling Company went bankrupt the next year. It was bought out by the R. T. Davis Milling Company, whose CEO, Davis himself, wanted to take this character to the next level.

Davis sought out a suitably maternal black woman to portray Aunt Jemima in person, and he found what he was looking for in Nancy Green. After being supplied with an apron and a bandanna, Green took the stage at the 1893 Chicago World's Fair as Aunt Jemima. There she demonstrated the proper use of "her" pancake mix for crowds of thousands. Audiences responded to her natural geniality and warmth, and the R. T. Davis Milling Company received more than fifty thousand orders for Aunt Jemima's instant pancake mix.

To give the icon more depth, the company devised a backstory for her. Aunt Jemima was a cook on a Louisiana plantation, famous for her fabulously fluffy and delicious pancakes. Many had tried to weasel the recipe out of her, but only the R. T. Davis Milling Company had succeeded.

Nancy Green portrayed Aunt Jemima until 1923, when she was killed in a car accident in Chicago. Due to money issues unrelated to this tragedy, the R. T. Davis Milling Company sold the rights to Aunt Jemima and her pancake mix to Quaker Oats in 1926.

Following Green's death, many different women nationwide stepped into the apron and bandanna. The last, Rosie Lee Moore Hall, was granted the position in 1950; she played the part until her death in 1967. At that point, Quaker Oats retired the concept of the living icon, bringing an end to an advertising campaign that had lasted seventy-four years.

The NAACP has protested the use of the Aunt Jemima icon since the early 1900s and called for a full boycott in 1965. In 1989 Quaker Oats updated Aunt Jemima's logo appearance, replacing the bandanna and apron with a modern hairdo and a set of pearl earrings. This was intended to remove her from her beginnings as a cook on a plantation, but for some this gesture is not enough. There is currently an online petition for the complete removal of Aunt Jemima as a logo. Quaker Oats has not responded to this protest, apparently comfortable that Aunt Jemima is an invitation to family breakfast, not a racist symbol.

Q Is there any duck in duck sauce?

A If you want to keep things authentic, the question should be, "Are there any plums in plum sauce?" because duck sauce is a nickname that plum sauce adopted over time. However, when speaking of Chinese food, there seems to be little authenticity left.

Yong Chen, a history professor at the University of California-Irvine, says that Chinese food "is quintessentially American." Ever since the first Chinese restaurants opened in California mining towns in the mid-nineteenth century, Chinese restaurateurs have looked for ways to Americanize their dishes. In China, and in American fine-dining establishments that serve Peking duck, the traditional sauce that accompanies this dish is hoisin sauce (which is soy-based), not plum sauce.

However, over time it became acceptable in the United States for plum sauce to be served with duck. Eventually—and quite logically—it took on the name duck sauce. Ed Schoenfeld, a restaurateur and Chinese food consultant, says that the Chinese condiment degraded over time as it became mass produced.

Duck sauce is not the only Americanized fare on a Chinese restaurant menu: General Tso's chicken was once very savory, made with garlic and vinegar. Today it is a batter-fried, syrup-laden shadow of its former self. Chop suey and crab rangoon, as well as sweet-and-sour pork, chicken, beef, and shrimp, are other dishes that are Chinese in name only. Even the fortune cookie was an idea that started in America, though it is now popular in China. Go figure.

For your further enlightenment, here is a list of common ingredients found in duck (plum) sauce: plums, vinegar, sugar, ginger, garlic, chiles, salt, and water. Nope, no duck.

Chapter Six

SPORTS

Q Who is Uncle Charlie?

A No, Uncle Charlie isn't the guy who gives you a roll of quarters for your birthday every year. In fact, when it comes to baseball, Uncle Charlie isn't a person at all—it's a nickname for the good old-fashioned pitch known as the curveball.

The legendary curveball relies on tight spin to create a sharp downward or sideward turn just as the ball reaches home plate. Many historians credit William Arthur "Candy" Cummings with inventing the popular pitch in the 1860s. As the story goes, the teenage Cummings noticed that by using certain wrist movements, he could manipulate the path of a clamshell as he flung it into the ocean. He tried these same techniques on a baseball, and after some trial and error the ball curved in the air—even when Cummings pitched underhanded, as required by the rules of baseball at the time. Cummings pitched professionally for a decade, baffling batters with his ball-busting creation.

Today, Cummings' curveball boasts many different nicknames, including the hammer, the hook, the deuce, and even the yakker. But why Uncle Charlie? Unfortunately, the answer remains shrouded in mystery. Paul Dickson's *The New Dickson Baseball Dictionary* claims the name derives from citizens band (CB) radio lingo of the 1970s; Uncle Charlie was a common nickname for the Federal Communications Commission (FCC) among CB broadcasters. How this became connected to the curveball is anyone's guess, although the accepted theory attributes it to phonetic similarities between the words "Charlie" and "curve."

Whatever its origin, Uncle Charlie remains a popular term to this day. Former major league pitcher Dwight Gooden's curve was so good, it was nicknamed Lord Charles. (Players have personified several other pitches, most notably the split-finger fastball, known to many as Mr. Splitty.) So the next time someone offers to introduce you to Uncle Charlie, don't set another place at the dinner table—put on a catcher's mitt, and keep your eye on the ball.

Q Why do golfers hate to putt?

A Most golfers hate to putt, at some level. Sometimes at a very visible, sweaty level. Even though golfers know it's possible to screw up every single shot from tee to green, putting is what winds up freaking them out.

Why? The easy answer is that putting is hard. Even for the pros. "I play along every year waiting for one week, maybe two, when I can putt," says Larry Nelson. And Nelson has been one of the best putters in professional golf for almost three decades.

We amateurs tend to think that pros make almost all of their putts. In fact, they miss at least six out of every hundred from two feet—an astonishingly high number. They make no more than one in every six putts from twenty feet. All we do is make things worse by imagining it's easier for the pros than it is.

And this gets us closer to the heart of the matter. Golfers tend to think too much, especially on the green.

"*Happy Gilmore* is a pretty good instructional film," says PGA teaching pro Peter Donahue. He explains that the loopy Adam Sandler character has the most vital trait in a good putter: He's happy to putt. "Golfers train themselves not to love to shoot but to be afraid to miss," Donahue says. "It's like Red Auerbach said in basketball: 'I don't care if you miss, just don't be afraid to shoot.'"

The best putters in the world are touring and teaching pros, obviously. But the next best, according to Donahue, are beginners. Why? It goes back to that thinking thing. Beginners don't ponder—they just putt.

After searching far and wide, we did uncover at least one person who likes to putt: PGA golfer Ben Crenshaw. "From the very beginning I enjoyed putting," he says in his autobiography. "I loved putting because it was just plain fun, and it fascinated me to watch the ball roll over those blades of grass."

Crenshaw, of course, is in the minority. Take it from Larry Eimers, a sports psychologist from Durham, North Carolina, who has counseled many a tortured putter: "You're in a risk area where you're liable to suffer humiliation or embarrassment if you miss it. …Everyone hates [the short] putt, because if you make it, no one gives a damn, but if you miss it, everyone raises their eyebrows. In the end, you're working eighteen holes to avoid humiliation."

Did we mention that golfers hate to putt?

Q Why is a marathon 26.2 miles?

A To most of us, running a marathon is incomprehensible. Driving 26.2 miles is perhaps a possibility, though only if we stop at least once for Fritos. Equally incomprehensible is the number itself, 26.2. Why isn't a marathon 26.4 miles? Or 25.9? Why, oh why, is the magic number 26.2?

To answer this curious question, we must examine the history of the marathon. Our current marathon is descended from a legend about the most famous runner in ancient Greece, a soldier named Philippides (his name was later corrupted in text to Pheidippides). For much of the fifth century BC, the Greeks were at odds with the neighboring Persian Empire; in 490 BC, the mighty Persians, led by Darius I, attacked the Greeks at the city of

Marathon. Despite being badly outnumbered, the Greeks managed to fend off the Persian troops (and ended Darius's attempts at conquering Greece).

After the victory, the legend holds, Philippides ran in full armor from Marathon to Athens—about twenty-five miles—to announce the good news. After several hours of running through the rugged Greek countryside, he arrived at the gates of Athens crying, "Rejoice, we conquer!" as Athenians rejoiced. Philippides then fell over dead. Despite a great deal of debate about the accuracy of this story, the legend still held such sway in the Greek popular mind that when the modern Olympic Games were revived in Athens in 1896, a long-distance running event known as a "marathon" was instituted.

How did the official marathon distance get to be 26.2 miles if the journey of Philippides was about twenty-five? In the first two Olympic Games, the "Philippides distance" was indeed used. But things changed in 1908, when the Olympic Games were held in London. The British Olympic committee determined that the marathon route would start at Windsor Castle and end in front of the royal box in front of London's newly built Olympic Stadium, a distance that happened to measure 26 miles, 385 yards.

There was no good reason for the whims of British lords to become the standard, but 26.2 somehow got ingrained in the sporting psyche. By the 1924 Olympics in Paris, this arbitrary distance had become the standard for all marathons.

Today, winning a marathon—heck, even completing one—is considered a premier athletic accomplishment. In cities such as Boston, New York, and Chicago, thousands of professionals and amateurs turn out to participate. Of course, wiser people remember what happened to Philippides when he foolishly tried to run such a long distance. Pass the Fritos.

Q What is cauliflower ear?

A First things first, people: If you're going to name a malady or a disease, for goodness sake, don't name it after food. It's unsettling. Some of us like to eat cauliflower, but then we come across a reference to cauliflower ear, we get a little curious, and the next thing we know, we're looking at disgusting pictures of actual human ears that, much to our dismay, really do look like cauliflower.

Because that's what happens with cauliflower ear: The ear kind of puffs up and takes on a curdled look not unlike that of cauliflower. It can happen to anybody who suffers an injury to their outer ear; wrestlers, boxers, and martial artists who don't wear protective headgear are particularly susceptible.

Bleeding between the ear's cartilage and skin results in swelling. The skin can turn pale or purple. If cauliflower ear is not treated in a timely manner, the cartilage will be deprived of nutrients and the condition can become permanent, with little hope of returning the ear to the original shape that we all prefer to see on the sides of peoples' heads.

The remedy for cauliflower ear is fairly simple: Blood is drained from the ear and any infection is treated. Boiling, steaming, and butter are not necessary.

Q Why is a football shaped that way?

A Would you rather call it a bladder? Because that's what footballs were made of before mass-produced rubber or leather balls became the norm.

The origins of the ball and the game can be traced to the ancient Greeks, who played something called harpaston. As in football, players scored by kicking, passing, or running over the opposition's goal line. The ball in harpaston was often made of a pig's bladder. This is because pigs' bladders were easy to find, round-ish in shape, relatively simple to inflate and seal, and fairly durable. (If you think playing ball with an internal organ is gross, consider what the pig's bladder replaced: a human head.)

Harpaston evolved into European rugby, which evolved into American football. By the time the first "official" football game was played at Rutgers University in New Jersey in the fall of 1869, the ball had evolved, too. To make the ball more durable and consistently shaped, it was covered with a protective layer that was usually made of leather.

Still, the extra protection didn't help the pig's bladder stay permanently inflated, and there was a continuous need to reinflate the ball. Whenever play was stopped, the referee unlocked the

ball—yes, there was a little lock on it to help keep it inflated—
and a player would pump it up.

Footballs back then were meant to be round, but the sphere was
imperfect for a couple reasons. First, the bladder lent itself more
to an oval shape; even the most perfectly stitched leather covering couldn't force the bladder to remain circular. Second, as a
game wore on, players got tired and were less enthused about
reinflating the ball. As a result, the ball would flatten out and take
on more of an oblong shape. The ball was easier to grip in that
shape, and the form slowly gained popularity, particularly after
the forward pass was introduced in 1906.

Through a series of rule changes relating to its shape, the football
became slimmer and ultimately developed its current look. And
though it's been many decades since pigs' bladders were relieved
of their duties, the football's nickname—a "pigskin"—lives on.

Q Why do baseball players wear knickers?

A Some call them knickers. Others call them short pants.
Either way, there's nothing short about the answer, which
stretches about one hundred and fifty years into the past. Back
then, baseball was evolving into a professional sport, and
there was a lot of innovation going on regarding the game's
equipment. This included pants.

The long, baggy—almost dressy—pants that players wore in
the mid-eighteen hundreds proved suboptimal where a player's

speed and agility were concerned. They simply got in the way. Some players innovated by having buttons sewn at the hem so the pant legs could be cinched tight. Other teams had straps on their pants. The Cincinnati Redlegs cut to the chase in 1868 by showing up one April day in honest-to-god knickers—the better to show off their red stockings, too.

Incidentally, this wasn't the only innovation the Redlegs brought to baseball. One year later, the Redlegs became the first openly all-professional baseball team. A year after that, their catcher invented the baseball glove—or at least became the first prominent ballplayer to use one.

The concept of a professional ballplayer has evolved since those days, and so have gloves—enormously. But interestingly, knickers stayed the norm for almost a century, until near the mid-twentieth century, when Carl Hubbell, Ted Williams, and others started to wear their pants in the "low-roll" style—that is, rolled into their uniform stockings around midcalf. It's entertaining to imagine the stir that caused, especially when we think of the disapproval that current-day heel-length trousers elicit from baseball purists. Ballplayers have always been vain about their pants, apparently.

Today, pant legs are all over the board. Some players wear them Redlegs style, right under the knee. Others wear them like the ballplayers of one hundred and fifty years ago, down to the ankle (but these are a good deal more form fitting on the way down the leg). Major League Baseball's 2002 collective bargaining agreement stipulates no pants past the tip of the shoe heel, for some measure of neatness in appearance. But the fact is, pant length is one of the areas of true sartorial creativity in baseball today, whether a player chooses to wear knickers or not.

Q Why do most sports go counterclockwise?

A For most nonathletes living their quiet day-to-day lives, doing things clockwise seems pretty intuitive. Doorknobs turn clockwise, screws are tightened clockwise, and yes, clocks run clockwise. Board games usually move clockwise, blackjack dealers hand out cards clockwise, and people in restaurants usually take turns ordering in a clockwise direction.

Yet in many of our sports, such as baseball and all types of racing, play moves in a counterclockwise direction. This can cause some serious confusion for clockwise-oriented individuals—just ask any T-ball coach trying to shepherd a young hitter down the first-base line.

How did this counterintuitive situation come to be? Part of the answer is rooted in history. In ancient times, when the Roman Empire ruled virtually the entire known Western world, a popular form of entertainment was chariot racing. As Charlton Heston fans know, chariot racing moved in a counterclockwise direction.

Roman horses were invaluable in war and were trained to turn to the left to give right-handed spear-wielding riders an advantage in battle; in the Circus Maximus, it was natural to build the track to suit this. Considering the power of habit in human social development, it seems reasonable to assume that future forms of racing simply adopted the same direction of travel as the mighty Romans.

Some science-minded individuals postulate that foot racing goes counterclockwise due to physical forces. Because most people are right-handed (and right-footed), a counterclockwise motion tends to help those with a dominant right leg speed around turns. This is because of centrifugal force, which we're sure everybody remembers from high school physics. For those who have forgotten, centrifugal force is that sense of momentum—called inertia—that tries to keep you going in a straight line when you're trying to turn. A right-legged individual moving counterclockwise, this theory argues, will have a better chance of counteracting this force.

Some sports move the other way. In England, for example, horse races travel in a clockwise direction. This seems particularly baffling, considering that American horse racing—which was brought over by the British during colonial times—moves counterclockwise. It turns out, though, that counterclockwise horse racing actually developed in the United States in response to the British tradition.

One of the first American horse tracks built after the Revolutionary War was established in 1780 by Kentuckian William Whitley. Flushed with pride at the newly won independence of the colonies, Whitley declared that horse racing in the new country should go in the opposite direction of those stodgy, tyrannical Brits.

Baseball, in which runners move counterclockwise around the bases, also may have descended from a British ancestor. Some baseball historians have postulated that the modern national pastime may be based on a British bat-and-ball game called rounders. Interestingly, rounders players moved in a clockwise direction around the bases; why this was reversed in the rules of baseball is not known.

Possibly, the counterclockwise movement has to do with the orientation of the diamond. It's far easier for righthanders to throw across the diamond to first base if the runner is moving in a counterclockwise direction (which is also why you almost never see lefthanders playing any infield positions except for first base).

Of course, from one perspective, clockwise and counter-clockwise are meaningless terms. Some physicists enjoy pointing out (somewhat smugly, we might add) that direction is entirely relative. Which means that those seemingly confused T-ball toddlers might be a lot smarter than we think.

Chapter Seven

WEIRD SCIENCE AND TECHNOLOGY

Q Why are Mexican jumping beans so jumpy?

A Mexican jumping beans don't really pull off the spectacular acrobatics you see in cartoons—and, sadly, they don't wear sombreros, grow moustaches, or shoot guns in the air, either. But they do move of their own accord, which ain't bad for a bean.

Of course, there's a catch: Mexican jumping beans aren't really beans at all. They're actually seed capsules with a squirmy moth larva inside.

In the spring, the jumping bean moth, affectionately known as *Cydia deshaisiana*, lays its eggs on the flower of the jumping bean shrub (*Sebastiana pavoniana*). The larvae hatch and dig into the developing soft capsules around the shrub's seeds. As each capsule grows and hardens, the larva relaxes safely inside, snacking on the seed.

This parasitic behavior keeps the capsule from doing what it's supposed to—spreading the shrub's seed to grow more shrubs. But the shrub produces enough seed capsules that moth larvae don't take over all of them. Both species are fully able to continue their reproductive cycles.

The hardened capsules fall off the shrub, and each breaks into several pieces called carpels, some of which have a larva inside. The larva spins thread on the inside of the carpel and can actually move the capsule by gripping the thread and banging its head into the side of the capsule. It does this as an instinctive reaction to heat—when you warm a jumping bean in your hand, you'll feel it squirm. It's unclear why the larvae do this, but it may be to move the carpel out of the hot sun into cooler areas.

In any case, if you warm a jumping bean in your hand and set it on a table, you might see it shift around a bit. But there's not exactly any *jumping* going on. It's enough movement to make the beans a popular novelty item, though. In the desert Rio Mayo region of Mexico where jumping bean moths and shrubs live, locals gather up the seed pods to be sold all over the world. In desert regions of Arizona, a similar species of moth burrows into the seedpods of a similar shrub, but most jumping beans come from Mexico around the city of Alamos, the "Jumping Bean Capital of the World."

So what happens to the larva next? Before it enters the pupal stage and turns into a moth, it chews an exit door into the side of the carpel, then blocks it up again with a silk thread plug. The adult moth has no teeth so it's up to the larva to prepare this easy trapdoor ahead of time.

The following spring, the moth emerges from its pupal case and pushes through the trapdoor. If the moth finds itself in its native habitat, it fulfills its lifelong destiny of mating with another moth, laying eggs on a jumping bean shrub, and dying in peace. But if the novelty trade has taken it far from home, where there are no jumping bean moths or jumping bean shrubs, it emerges to find that it has spent a year crammed in a pod for nothing. If it *could* jump around shooting guns in the air, would you blame it? That's a raw deal.

Q How do those transparent TelePrompTers work?

A For those of you too busy watching Cartoon Network to be bothered with distractions like the State of the Union address, the technology in question is the seemingly transparent panes of glass flanking the president during a speech. Though this style of TelePrompTer has been used in other events, it has become so synonymous with speeches given by the president that it is colloquially known as a "presidential TelePrompTer."

What kind of sorcery can deliver the content of a speech to a speaker without being seen by the audience?

While these TelePrompTers look like they're from the future, they are actually a modification of the type of system that is used in just about every TV newscast. With normal TelePrompTers, a monitor is placed perpendicular to the lens of a camera that displays the text the anchor reads. Then a half-silvered mirror—a piece of glass or plastic with a very thin reflective layer on one side, similar to the one-way mirror you'd find in an interrogation room—is placed at an angle in front of the camera lens and above the monitor. The mirror reflects the words on the monitor to the speaker but is transparent to the camera. The result is the illusion that the newscaster is staring directly into the camera, delivering line after line of flawless copy, apparently from memory.

The presidential TelePrompTer is a slight modification of this method. For this setup, two flat-screen LCD monitors are placed on the podium; they reflect the text upward onto two treated squares of glass that are like the aforementioned half-silvered mirror.

The next time you see a speech in which a presidential TelePrompTer is used, notice how the glass is tilted toward the podium to catch the monitor's reflections instead of away from the speaker—it's the opposite of how a music stand, for instance, would be positioned to hold a sheet of paper. The result is that the glass panels appear blank to the audience while the speaker sees the reflected text from the LCD monitors. The glass is placed on both sides of the president so that our fearless leader won't miss a beat while "naturally" turning left and right to address both sides of the room.

So it's not magic at all, just boring old science. Sorry. Now you know why magicians never reveal the secrets behind their tricks.

Q If the Professor on *Gilligan's Island* can make a radio out of a coconut, why can't he fix a hole in a boat?

A Those of you under the age of twenty-five might be staring blankly at this page and saying to yourself, "What the heck is *Gilligan's Island*?" Trust us—it was a television show, and a very popular one at that.

Gilligan's Island aired on CBS from 1964 to 1967 (and then *ad infinitum* on TBS, TNT, and Nick at Nite), and was based on a simple premise: A motley group of people on a "three-hour tour" are shipwrecked on a deserted island. One of these shipwrecked tourists was Roy "the Professor" Hinkley, a man with six college degrees and advanced knowledge of technology, science, and obscure island languages. Over the course of ninety-eight episodes, the Professor was able to create radios, lie detectors, telescopes, sewing machines, and other gadgets out of little more than a few coconuts and some bamboo. In short, the Professor was the MacGyver of his era. (What? You don't know about the main characters on that show either? We are getting old. Okay, think of *Gilligan's Island* as a goofy precursor to *Lost*.)

With all of Hinkley's technological wizardry, the question must be asked: Why couldn't the Professor fix a simple boat? (Fortunately, most of the male viewers were too concerned with staring at Mary Ann and Ginger to think logically.) The answer, of course, was ratings. Though *Gilligan's Island* was never a smash hit, it was popular enough to last for several seasons. As anybody can tell you, if the Professor was able to fix the boat, there would be no show.

As it turns out, the Professor and his friends had to wait more than a decade to be rescued. Since CBS canceled the 1968 season of *Gilligan's Island* at the last minute, the final episode of the 1967 season found the crew still stranded on its island. In 1978, a special two-part made-for-TV movie, titled *Rescue from Gilligan's Island*, detailed the crew's long-awaited rescue.

It is only fitting that even after a decade, the Professor wasn't able to figure out simple boat repair. Instead, the castaways tied their huts together to make a raft, and they floated to freedom, where they presumably spent the rest of their lives watching reruns of themselves on cable television.

Q Are there robots that feel love?

A This question has long been fodder for science fiction. And if it has you dreaming of a day when a robot takes your hand, leans over, and whispers sweet nothings in your ear, you might want to push your internal "pause" button. That day isn't quite ready to dawn.

For now, robots can only react to, mirror, or even intuit our behavior. In Japan, one life-size robot, Kansei, can mimic thirty-six expressions, including those of anger, fear, sadness, happiness, surprise, and disgust. When Kansei hears the word love, it smiles. Japan believes that hastening the development of robots like Kansei is crucial for its society. For instance, these machines can help care for the elderly, who represent one-fifth of the country's population. According to the cadre of artificial intelligence engineers, making robots more effective and omnipresent in society calls for sophisticated versions that can grasp emotions, as well as learn and feel for themselves.

Will these feelings ever include love? British writer David Levy, author of the book *Love + Sex with Robots*, claims that at the very least robots will become more "sexed up" in the coming fifty years. Advanced robot design, he says, will include serving humankind's more carnal desires. As a self-proclaimed augur of robot-human relations, Levy espouses that, like prostitutes or sex dolls, robots will present convincing simulations of love. In addition, he asserts that robots will provide companionship. Even marriage to robots will be possible. This is good news for those of you who haven't had a date since Clinton was in office.

While the notion of a honeymoon in Paris with a robot may seem outlandish, don't be too quick to eschew it. Even though the jury is still out on whether robots will ever love humans, it's been established that humans can feel powerful emotions toward robots, says *New Scientist* magazine.

For instance, U.S. soldiers serving in Iraq felt a unique kinship with Packbots and Talon robots, which dispose of bombs and locate landmines; some soldiers felt profound sadness when these robots were destroyed in explosions. Duke University students name and dress their robotic Roomba vacuums. Some even relate to their Roomba as if it were a family member.

Until the day those Roombas and other robots like them can reciprocate such feelings, we'll need to find love among ourselves. And that seems to be every bit as tricky and elusive as programming the emotion into a machine. Take it from comedienne Lily Tomlin, who said, "If love is the answer, could you please rephrase the question?"

Q What is the crap cannon?

A Picture this: An angry mob descends upon Washington, D.C. Fed up with gas prices, water shortages, and the quality of network TV programming, the crowd marches ominously toward the Capitol. Just as the situation is about to turn ugly, officers in riot gear scramble into position. They're armed with a strange new weapon. After one last futile vocal warning, they aim and fire.

Not a sound is heard, but waves of protesters stop suddenly in their tracks. Strange looks come over their faces. Some squint. Others stare dreamily into the distance. Many fall to the ground, while others squat or cross their legs. A few grasp desperately for any available reading material.

A potentially violent and disastrous encounter has been narrowly averted, thanks to the crap cannon, the government's latest, greatest weapon for crowd control. Also known as the "Brown Note," it uses infrasonic waves to force its unsuspecting victims into that most debilitating of states: the uncontrollable movement of their bowels.

Sound far-fetched? That's probably because it is. The crap cannon is a bit of fiction dreamed up by someone—either paranoid political activists or deranged police officials. But reports of its alleged existence spread like wildfire in the months leading up to the 2008 Democratic Convention in Denver.

This sort of serious silliness is not unprecedented. Rumors of bizarre new weapons occasionally crop up, and sometimes those rumors aren't entirely unfounded. In 2004, a watchdog group uncovered evidence that the U.S. military was investigating the use of a "gay bomb" that when detonated would instantly transform soldiers into homosexuals (assuming, of course, that they weren't already homosexuals). Why? The half-cocked theory went like this: The targeted soldiers would soon be too busy engaging in hot lovemaking to be bothered with all that nasty fighting.

Your tax dollars hard (ahem) at work.

But back to the crap cannon. At first, it almost sounds legitimate. But if you think it through, its efficacy seems dubious. For one thing, if you're an angered, dangerous rioter, does a little poop in your pants really make you any less bent on destruction? Not to mention that the crap cannon would help to supply its targets with their own pungent ammunition: During the 1968 Democratic Convention in Chicago, rioters were seen throwing bags of human feces at the cops who were pummeling them.

Imagine the aftereffects. The officers processing the inevitable arrests wouldn't need booking rooms—they'd need changing stations. And we don't even want to contemplate what sort of horrific mess would result from using the crap cannon and the gay bomb simultaneously.

Besides, we can think of a far better use for this technology. Those of us who occasionally indulge in a diet devoid of fiber and loaded with good stuff like meat, cheese, pasta, and pastries would welcome an occasional shot from the ol' crap cannon. It might even make the perfect Father's Day gift.

Q Why does a seashell sound like the ocean?

A Is that big spiral conch you picked up during last year's trip to Hawaii still whispering sweet nothings in your ear? Well, that isn't the roar of the blue Pacific you hear—it's nothing more than the barrage of ambient noise around you.

Ah, science can be so harshly unsentimental sometimes! Seashells don't really create any sound all by themselves. Inside, they're a labyrinth of hollow areas and hard, curved surfaces that happen to be really good reflectors of racket.

When you hold a seashell up to your ear, that shell is actually capturing and amplifying all the little noises occurring around you. These noises are usually so hushed that you don't even hear them unless you're paying very close attention. However, when they begin bouncing off the cavity of a shell, the echoes resonate more loudly into your ear. And what do you know? They sound a lot like ocean waves rolling up to shore.

It doesn't matter how far away you are from the sea, or even if you have a seashell. You can re-create the same "ocean sound" effect by simply cupping your hand, or a coffee mug, over your ear. Just be sure that mug is empty—or you'll really hear a splash.

Q Can you get cancer from your cell phone?

A This question has come up time and again since 1993, when a man claimed on national television that the radiation from his wife's cell phone caused her to develop cancer. He filed a lawsuit against the manufacturer of the phone, but the case was dismissed due to a lack of evidence.

Seven years later, a neurologist in Baltimore brought a similar suit against his cell phone's manufacturer, alleging that extensive use of his cell phone led to cancer of the brain. Given the magnitude of the case—he sought eight hundred million dollars in damages—it stirred up quite a bit of media attention, and the furor was only fueled by his profession, since it seemed to make his lawsuit all the more credible. Further compounding the issue was an episode of *Larry King Live*, in which an epidemiologist suggested that there might be a link between cell phone use and cancer.

These events were quite sensational, and have continued to resurface in the media every so often. What frequently is overlooked, however, is that researchers have found no clear connection between cell phone use and cancer. It's certainly true that cellular phones emit small levels of radiofrequency radiation. However, the good news is that the amount is not only miniscule, but also has not been found to cause, advance, or contribute to existing cancerous growths.

Plus, as cell phone technology improves, newer models produce less and less radiofrequency radiation. And if that weren't enough, both the Food and Drug Administration (FDA) and Federal Communications Commission (FCC) limit the amount of radiofrequency radiation that a cell phone can emit—so even if a phone could theoretically produce enough to be harmful, it would never make it to the market.

Although the FCC has safeguards in place regarding radio-frequency regulation, the question of safety comes up often enough to warrant a disclaimer: The FCC does acknowledge that there are potential risks associated with the use of cellular devices, and advises those concerned with radiation to take the simple step of increasing the distance between the body and the source of the radiation. Since it's the cell phone that generates the radiation, one can simply use a headset or a Bluetooth earpiece to keep the phone at a distance from the head (and therefore the brain), thereby reducing exposure.

So go ahead: Breathe a sigh of relief, and go right back to your cell phone conversations. You're not in any real danger of developing cancer as a result, no matter how long you spend with the phone pressed to your ear.

Q How come underwater tunnels don't collapse?

A Ever dig a hole at the beach? Just when you think you're finally going to get all the way to China, the walls collapse and your whole hole disappears. (Which, incidentally, is why you should never let children dig at the beach unsupervised.) The length of time your walls will hold up before caving in is known to sandhogs as the "stand-up" time.

Who are sandhogs? They're not little animals burrowing into the sand; they're the men and women who earn their livings in tunnel construction, and they wear the name proudly. Tunnel digging is a high-risk job, and sandhogs obviously have a vested interest in the stand-up time of mud walls, especially when they're digging an underwater tunnel. How exactly can you dig a tunnel through the wet, soggy mud at the bottom of a river without courting certain disaster?

Back in 1818, English engineer Marc Isambard Brunel asked this same question. While strolling on the London docks one day, he noticed a shipworm, a.k.a. *teredo navalis,* boring through some rotting timbers. How did the tiny worm make a tunnel without getting crushed? Close inspection revealed that the worm used its hard, shell-like head as a shield. As the worm ate into the wood like an excavating shovel, its head moved forward, making a tunnel large enough for its body to pass through.

Brunel built himself a cast-iron shield shaped like the head of the worm, only his was two stories high and had several doors for mouths. A worker standing behind the shield would excavate earth through a door. As a hollow space was created in front of the shield, a set of jacks pressed the iron frame forward a few inches at a time, leaving a smooth section of earth where the rim of shield had been. Instantly, bricklayers would get to work, reinforcing this mud wall before it caved in.

As you may guess, this was a slow process. It took Brunel eighteen years to complete a 1,506-foot tunnel beneath London's River Thames. His shield method worked, however, and parts of his tunnel, which opened in 1843, are still in use today.

Though there are several new ways to construct underwater tunnels, including a tunnel–boring machine and prefabricated submersible tubing, the principle behind Brunel's shield continues to be employed in subterranean construction projects.

What is the world's longest underwater tunnel? The Seikan Tunnel, which runs under Japan's Tsugaru Strait, holds the record at 33.49 miles. But in April 2007, Russia announced plans to dig a tunnel to Alaska—a whopping sixty-four miles across the Bering Strait. Impossible? Not if you ask the sandhogs. They'll be there to dig that tunnel through rock, sand, silt, and mud. Just like they've dug all the others.

Q What causes red-eye in photographs?

A It can ruin pictures that are otherwise frame-worthy: two flaming-red pinpoints where the subject's eyes should be, turning a grinning child into something out of a horror movie. Pictures that would have been proudly displayed wind up hidden away—mementos of disappointment rather than pride.

Red-eye appears primarily at night or in darker rooms, in photographs taken with a flash. At night or in less-well-lighted rooms, the subject's retinas are open more often than in places with bright light, to allow for clearer vision in dimmer situations. When a shutterbug groups everyone together for a picture at the end of the day or in a dark room, the flash of his camera hits the wide-open retinas and fills them with light. The blood-rich retinas appear bright red when they are illuminated and photographed because the pupil is actually clear, even though it appears black when we look at someone's eyes. The flash of light is sent to the back of that person's eye, allowing us to see the retina, which is covered in blood vessels. (Young children with blue eyes are most susceptible to red-eye, according to Kodak.)

As a red-eye reduction feature, newer cameras will flash several times before taking a picture. Exposing the eye to bright light before the picture is snapped will cause the pupil to contract, thereby reducing the amount of light the retina reflects back to the camera and reducing the amount of red in the subject's eyes. Another helpful option is to turn on additional lights. Distance also plays a role—the closer you are, the less likely you are to have red-eye.

Knowing when red-eye will be most prevalent and what can be done to prevent it will ensure that your subjects look like humans when you get your prints back. That means more photos on the mantel and fewer in cardboard boxes, stacked in the closet, or slid under the bed.

Q What is Sir Thomas Crapper's claim to fame?

A It's only natural that some of life's greatest imponderables should occupy us while we are sitting on the toilet. "Why is the sky blue?" "Is there really a God?" "Who invented this thing I'm sitting on right now?"

Some people are familiar with the legend: Thomas Crapper, a Victorian-era plumber, invented the flush toilet. Queen Victoria was so delighted that she bestowed upon him a knighthood, while Sir Thomas bestowed upon his invention his last name, and to this day, it serves as a somewhat crass nickname for the toilet.

It's such a neat story that one wishes it were true. Though there really was a Victorian-era plumber named Thomas Crapper, he did not invent the flush toilet—in fact, it was invented in 1596, a couple hundred years before Crapper was born, by author and inventor Sir John Harington. Nor did Thomas Crapper receive a knighthood, incidentally, so there's no real reason to call him "Sir."

But what about his last name? Surely it's more than a coincidence that people often refer to the toilet as the "crapper." There is some evidence that Thomas did in fact lend his last name to bathroom lexicon. Though Crapper did not invent the toilet, he did sell a great deal of them in the late nineteenth century—and each had its tank emblazoned with the Crapper name. In World War I, American soldiers who encountered these toilets while stationed in Europe—some of the soldiers were seeing flush toilets for the first time!— simply started using poor Thomas's last name as a nickname for going to the bathroom.

Thomas did escape one ignominy, though: The word crap is not derived from his last name. Crap, meaning "the chaff of grain," first appeared in the Middle English language in the fifteenth century, well before Thomas Crapper's halcyon days, and was used to refer to excrement while young Thomas was still a boy.

Crapper merely had an unfortunate last name given his chosen profession. His is a saga that lends new meaning to the phrase "fifteen minutes of fame."

Q How does a flak jacket stop a bullet?

A "Flak" is an abbreviation of *Fliegerabwehrkanone*, a German word that looks rather silly (as many German words do). There's nothing silly, however, about its meaning: antiaircraft cannon.

Serious development of flak jackets began during World War II, when air force gunners wore nylon vests with steel plates sewn into them as protection against shrapnel. After the war, manu-facturers discovered that they could remove the steel plates and instead make the vests out of multiple layers of dense, heavily weaved nylon.

Without the heavy steel plates, the vests became a viable option for ground troops to wear during combat. Anywhere from sixteen to twenty-four layers of this nylon fabric were stitched together into a thick quilt. In the 1960s, DuPont developed Kevlar, a light-weight fiber that is five times stronger than a piece of steel of the same weight. Kevlar was added to flak jackets in 1975.

It seems inconceivable that any cloth could withstand the force of a bullet. The key, however, is in the construction of the fabric. In a flak jacket, the fibers are interlaced to form a super strong net. The fibers are twisted as they are woven, which adds to their density. Modern flak jackets also incorporate a coating of resin on the fibers and layers of plastic film between the layers of fabric. The result is a series of nets that are designed to bend but not break.

A bullet that hits the outer layers of the vest's material is flattened into a mushroomlike shape. The remaining layers of the vest can then dissipate the misshapen bullet's energy and prevent it from penetrating. The impact of the offending bullet usually leaves a bruise or blunt trauma to internal organs, which is a minor injury compared to the type of devastation a bullet is meant to inflict.

While no body armor is 100 percent impenetrable, flak jackets offer different levels of protection depending on the construction and materials involved. At the higher levels of protection, plates of lightweight steel or special ceramic are still used. But all flak jackets incorporate this netlike fabric as a first line of defense. *Fliegerabwehrkanone*, indeed.

Q Why doesn't glue stick to the inside of the glue bottle?

A We're going to presume that the glue we're talking about is standard, everyday school or stationary white glue. It gets more complicated, but we'll address that in a bit. The more appropriate name for something that sticks to things, and sticks things together, is "adhesive," by the way.

There are a couple of reasons that glue doesn't stick to the inside of the bottle. The first is that most glues begin to work as they dry out. They start off mixed with some kind of fluid (often water), and when they mix with air, the fluid eventually evaporates, leaving behind the hardened sticky molecules. Because the glue inside a bottle is not exposed to that much air, it stays in liquid form.

The other reason is that there are some materials that certain adhesives won't stick to because the chemical structures of those materials don't react with the adhesive. Generally, these are plastics. Keeping the glue from sticking to the inside of the bottle is a simple matter of making the bottle out of these stubbornly unsticky materials. Superglue tubes, for example, are generally made of the plastic polyethylene, although they may also be made out of aluminum.

The more complicated bit is that glue, as we mentioned, has many different forms. Tar is an adhesive, and so are substances like epoxy and thermoplastic. Many of these adhesives bond in different ways. Krazy Glue reacts to the presence of trace amounts of water and forms super-strong bonds. Many apparently dry surfaces have microscopic water droplets sticking to them, which is why the darned stuff seems to stick to everything. To keep Krazy Glue from being overzealous, you have to keep the tube dry.

Epoxy only works when two compounds that set off a reaction in each other are combined, so you merely need to keep them separated to prevent excessive stickiness. Heat-based adhesives, such as the thermoplastic glue used in glue guns, work by causing reactions through heat and then being allowed to harden; they won't stick if they're not heated up.

To sum it up, then, the glue doesn't stick to the inside of whatever container it's in because the manufacturers have gone to great lengths to prevent its stick-inducing elements from activating. How convenient for us.

Q Why do old ladies have blue hair?

A Black knee socks with sandals. Pants hiked to the armpits. Wraparound sunglasses enveloping half the face like something out of a low-budget science-fiction movie. As we get older, our hearing fails, our eyesight wanes, and our bodies crumble, but perhaps nothing collapses more dramatically than our sense of fashion. Some of these fashion abominations arise from practicality; others exist because older people simply don't care. But blue hair? Surely that's not by design, is it?

Don't worry—Grandma hasn't suddenly embraced punk culture. Ironically, though, while most style disasters of the elderly stem from fashion apathy, blue hair comes from trying too hard. As everyone knows, our hair turns gray as we age. That's because the hair's pigment cells, which produce the melanin that gives hair its color, don't live quite as long as the average human body. As the pigment cells die, the melanin dissipates, leaving the hair a silvery or white color.

Unfortunately, in our modern age, it also leaves the hair partially yellow, thanks to the decades of pollution and chemicals we have been subjected to. In order to combat this, many commercial rinses include a blue dye that, in theory, negates the yellowing and turns the hair a lovely silver color. However, these rinses sometimes have too much blue dye or are inappropriately applied, leaving the hair tinted blue and making Grandma look like she just emerged from a Ramones show at CBGB.

As with other fashion quirks of senior citizens, it's best to simply kiss Grandma on the cheek and compliment her on her new hairdo regardless of its hue. God willing, she doesn't even realize it's blue.

Q Will there be an elevator to outer space someday?

A Rockets are for suckers. Scientists at NASA looking for a cheaper way to build space stations and satellites have hit upon an idea that sounds ludicrous but that they swear is feasible: an elevator that reaches from Earth's surface to outer space.

"How could that be possible?" you ask. "What have these scientists been smoking?" The answer is nanotubes. (That's not what they've been smoking—it's the technology that could make a space elevator possible.) Discovered in 1991, nanotubes are cylindrical carbon molecules that make steel look like a ninety-eight-pound weakling. A space elevator's main component would be a sixty-thousand-odd-mile nanotube ribbon, measuring about as thin as a sheet of paper and about three feet wide.

It gets weirder. That ribbon would require a counterweight up at the top to keep it in place. The counterweight, hooked to the nanotube ribbon, would be an asteroid pulled into Earth's orbit or a satellite. Once secured, the ribbon would have moving platforms attached to it. Each platform would be powered by solar-energy-reflecting lasers and could carry several thousand tons of cargo up to the top. The trip would take about a week. Transporting materials to outer space in this fashion would supposedly reduce the cost of, say, putting a satellite into orbit from about ten thousand dollars a pound to about one hundred dollars a pound.

The base of the elevator would be a platform situated in the eastern Pacific Ocean, near the equator, safe from hurricanes and many miles clear of commercial airline routes. The base would be mobile so that the whole thing could be moved out of the path of potentially damaging space junk orbiting Earth. Although there are a lot of theoretical kinks to work out, the more optimistic of the scientists who have hatched this scheme believe the whole thing could be a reality within a couple of decades. Think about that the next time you step into an elevator and chug on up to the third floor.

Q What is the slowest-moving object in the world?

A Jet cars and supersonic airplanes get all the glory for their high-speed records, but there are some objects that are just as notable for their amazing slowness. In fact, they go so slowly that scientists need special equipment to detect their movement. What moves slowest of all? The answer just might be right under your feet.

The surface of the earth is covered by tectonic plates, rigid slabs made of the planet's crust and the brittle uppermost mantle below, called the lithosphere. Some of the plates are enormous, and each is in constant movement—shifting, sliding, or colliding with other plates or sliding underneath to be drawn back down into the deep mantle. The plates "float" on the lower mantle, or asthenosphere; the lower mantle is not a liquid, but it is subjected to heat and pressure, which softens it so that it can flow very, very slowly.

When an earthquake occurs, parts of the plates can move very suddenly. Following the Great Alaska Earthquake in 1964, America's largest ever, the two plates involved shifted about thirty feet by the end of the event. However, most of the time tectonic plates move relatively steadily and very slowly. Scientists use a technique called Satellite Laser Ranging (SLR) to detect their movement.

SLR relies on a group of stations spread around the world that use lasers to send extremely short pulses of light to satellites equipped with special reflective surfaces. The time it takes for the light to make the roundtrip from the satellite's main reflector is instantaneously measured. According to the U.S. Geological Survey, this collection of measurements "provides instantaneous range measurements of millimeter level precision" that can be used in numerous scientific applications. One of those applications is measuring the movement of the earth's tectonic plates over time.

How slow do tectonic plates move? The exact speed varies: The slowest plates move at about the same rate of speed that your fingernails grow, and the fastest plates go at about the same rate that your hair grows. A rough range is one to thirteen centimeters per year. The fastest plates are the oceanic plates, and the slowest are the continental plates. At the moment, the Slowest Object Award is a tie between the Indian and Arabian plates, which are moving only three millimeters per year.

If you're wondering who the runner-up is in the race to be slowest, it appears to be glaciers. The slowest glaciers creep a few inches each day, still faster than tectonic plates. However, some glaciers are so speedy they can cover nearly eight miles in a single year, and sometimes a glacier can surge. In 1936, the Black Rapids Glacier in Alaska galloped toward a nearby lodge and highway, averaging fifty-three meters a day over three months. That leaves tectonic plates in the dust.

Chapter Eight

HISTORY

Q Did someone else write Shakespeare's plays?

A For someone so famous, William Shakespeare remains a mysterious figure. Here's what we know:

He was born in Stratford-upon-Avon, England, in 1564 and died in 1616. He married when he was eighteen, his wife bore three children, and he lived apart from his family in London. Shakespeare left behind scant personal correspondence, but he gave the world thirty-eight plays, 154 sonnets, and two narrative poems. Thirty-six of the plays were published seven years after his death in what is now called the *First Folio*. He wrote romances, histories, comedies, tragedies, and "problem plays" (which can't really be characterized by any of the previous categories). The man was incredibly talented.

Or was he? Conspiracy theorists have alleged through the years that Shakespeare didn't write any of his plays and that they were really penned by, among others, Edward de Vere (also known as the Earl of Oxford), Sir Francis Bacon, Christopher Marlowe, or even Queen Elizabeth I. One prominent theory is that there are anagrams in the plays that, when decoded, reveal an author other than Shakespeare. Another is that Shakespeare was too uneducated to have written so wonderfully and that he was merely a front for a female or noble author. (It was considered uncouth in those days for such an esteemed person to write plays.)

So we ask: Did Shakespeare write his own material? The answer is yes...and no.

Upon arriving in London sometime around 1588, Shakespeare joined a theater company called Lord Chamberlain's Men, later renamed the King's Men. Shakespeare's plays were performed almost exclusively by this company. He was an actor, too, and appeared in his own and in other company members' plays. The creation of a play was (and still is) a collaborative effort. Copies of scripts were shared, commented upon, and edited. Once rehearsals began, scenes were deleted and changed. Even after a play premiered, it was subject to change.

Plays were the best entertainment available to the public in an era without video games, movies, television, and iPods, but a company couldn't survive without constantly updating its offerings. As a result, there was enormous pressure for new material. And the plays were not actually owned by the playwright in the way we use a copyright today—the company owned the play. Shakespeare made his living by being a member of the company, not by writing any individual piece (although he was listed as the company's house playwright).

The point is, a number of people in the company would have provided input on Shakespeare's plays. That, however, is about as far as the conspiracy goes. Almost all academics today reject the notion that Shakespeare didn't write his plays, but as with shooters on the grassy knoll and UFOs in New Mexico, rumors persist in the popular mind. It's a plot device worthy of, well, Shakespeare.

Q Can Texas really split into five states if it wants to?

A The present-day answer is: It depends on whom you ask. But the truth of the matter is, the time that Texas could have amicably split into more than one state is long, long past.

Texas was annexed on February 28, 1845. On March 1, 1845, Congress approved the Joint Resolution for Annexing Texas to the United States. This document allowed Texas to split into four additional states plus the state of Texas, for a total of five states, if Texas wanted.

This was partly motivated by the sheer size of the sucker: Texas was four times bigger than Missouri, the largest state at the time. But there were other factors as well. The Missouri Compromise had established the boundaries for slavery based on latitude:

Above the 36°30′ N line, slavery was illegal; below it, slavery was legal. If Texas was one big state, it would have been a slave state, which would have significantly boosted the slave states' numbers. Both the North and the South viewed splitting Texas as potentially helpful. For the North, there was plenty of room above that latitude line for a free state or two, and the South saw plenty of space below the line for keeping slavery legal.

No one ever got around to actually splitting the state, however, and by the time the Civil War started, Texas (all of it) seceded from the Union to fight alongside the rest of the South. After that, the chances that Texas would be split in any way were very slim.

Following the Civil War, Texas was readmitted as a state. Article IV, Section 3 of the Constitution says that no state can be formed by using parts of established states without the approval of the state legislature and the approval of Congress. So really, with approval, any state or states can form "super states" or "mini states." The question is whether Texas could do this without the approval of Congress, based on the language in the original Joint Resolution. Many argue that because Texas had to be formally readmitted to the States after secession, the Joint Resolution for Annexing Texas is null and void. Others think its right to split itself is still viable.

These days, if Texas were to split into five states, Congress would need to add eight senators. And since Texas is a "red" state, this could certainly help the Republicans. But everyone would have to agree on the boundaries, names, and other characteristics of the extra states being created. Presumably, one of the pieces would get to be Texas, and the rest would have to find other names (East Texas, West Texas, South Texas, and North Texas, perhaps). When you start thinking about the specifics, and all the people who wouldn't want Texas to split (including plenty of Texans), the idea is too messy to ever become a reality.

Q How old does an item have to be to be considered an antique?

A Depends on whom you ask. Bet you knew we were going to say that.

The United States Customs Service classifies items that are at least one hundred years old as genuine antiques, at least for import purposes. Items of that age can be brought into the country duty free.

Some old-school purists claim that the term "antique" can only apply to things made before 1820. By that time, the Industrial Revolution was in full swing, and that year marks a point at which handcrafted items were being widely replaced by machine-made goods.

The word itself is closely related to the word "antiquities." At one point, "antiquities" meant "treasures from ancient times"—think Rome, Greece, Egypt, and Mesopotamia. Later on, the word "antique" took on different shades of meaning, conjuring images of the handmade items of a bygone age, lusted after and collected by people who didn't value factory-made stuff.

No doubt nostalgia has increased the prices of those pre-1820 handcrafted tables and plates, just as nostalgia plays a role today when we price and trade collectibles. Is Depression glass antique? How about Bakelite trinkets, or Howdy Doody lunchboxes? By the definitions above, no, they are not antiques.

Vintage, collectible, or antique: If collectors are willing to pay thousands of dollars for these objects, does it really matter what they are called?

Q How come Esperanto never caught on?

A Esperanto has fallen short of the hopes of its creator, L. L. Zamenhof, but it has by no means been a flop. When the Russian-born Zamenhof unveiled Esperanto in 1887, he envisioned it as a flexible world language that would become the shared tongue of governments everywhere and would promote peace and understanding. Although Esperanto never became that pervasive, for decades it has been the most used "model" or "constructed" language in the world, with estimates of current users ranging as high as two million. That's more than the speakers of many natural languages, such as those spoken by Native Americans, aboriginal populations on other continents, and European minority peoples.

According to estimates, there are a few hundred to about a thousand native speakers of Esperanto—folks whose parents taught them the language as a baby. Among these is gazillionaire Hungarian financier, activist, and philanthropist George Soros. Although Soros can stay in—or buy, for crying out loud—any hotel in the world, he can also use his Esperanto to secure lodgings with any other Esperantist in roughly ninety countries, one of the language's endearing features.

Tens of thousands of books have been published in Esperanto, including original and translated works; there are Esperanto television and radio broadcasts, magazines, and an annual world congress that attracts an average of two thousand attendees. Its proponents say it is up to twenty times easier to learn than other languages.

So why didn't Esperanto succeed on Zamenhof's terms? There are several reasons:

• Given the disparity of languages in the world, it is impossible to construct a vocabulary and grammar that doesn't pose serious challenges to someone.

• The language's sounds are too similar to Zamenof's native Belarussian, making pronunciation hard for many. Culturally speaking, it is European in its vocabulary and semantics.

• The vocabulary is unnecessarily large, due to the constant additions of new word roots rather than new words being based on old ones.

• Esperanto and its speakers have been the subject of persecution. It was outlawed in communist Russia until 1956, and Esperanto speakers have been killed under totalitarian regimes. Hitler claimed it could become the language of an international Jewish conspiracy, which was a testament to both Esperanto's success and Hitler's insanity.

But the biggest strike against the language is that it sprung from no shared natural culture. To grow large, a language needs a considerable group of people speaking together daily and developing close associations among their shared experiences and shared words. Languages are an outgrowth of human behavior and history, not the result of well-intentioned intellectual efforts. Put it this way: Any language whose biggest gabfest is an annual world congress isn't going to take over the world.

Still, Esperanto was and is a success. Consider this: Around the time Zamenhof was inventing Esperanto, a German priest, who was acting on something God told him in a dream, invented Volapük. The language got off to a fast start, but today it's estimated that only a few dozen people speak Volapük. Now that's a lonely world congress.

Q Did Catherine the Great die while having sex with a horse?

A Catherine II of Russia did not die while having sex with a stallion. The rumor that a harness broke mid-coitus and caused Catherine to be crushed beneath her massive sex partner is just that—a rumor, one that was particularly popular right after her death in 1796. But Catherine lived so large, and so boldly, and so powerfully that the average Russian *boyar* (noble) could be forgiven for believing it.

Catherine was not actually Russian, nor was she actually named Catherine. Rather, the woman we know as Catherine the Great of Russia was Sophie Fredericke Auguste von Anhalt-Zerbst, a minor German princess born in 1729 in the province of Stettin. Her marriage prospects weren't particularly good, and an attempt when she was fifteen to pair her up with the Grand Duke Peter of Russia initially failed.

But Princess Sophie was ambitious and determined. As a guest of Czar Peter II and his wife Elizabeth, she learned to speak Russian. She chose a new Russian name, Ekaterine Ekaterina, and she took instruction so that she could renounce the German Lutheran church and be welcomed into the Russian Orthodox Church. She was determined to marry the Grand Duke. The day after she was baptized, she did indeed marry him, and he was later crowned Emperor Peter III.

Peter was impotent, and the marriage may have remained unconsummated for at least twelve years. Peter took a mistress, but Catherine did better than that. She was believed to have had at least three lovers even before her husband was crowned tsar in 1762: Sergei Saltykov, Stanislaw Poniatowski, and Gregory Orlov. The year Peter III became tsar, he was deposed in a bloodless coup and was killed three days later by a courtier. Although there were rumors that Catherine and Orlov were involved in the coup—she did nothing to punish the murderers—no evidence was ever linked directly to her.

Catherine was crowned Empress Catherine II, although many assumed that she was only meant to hold the throne for her son Grand Duke Paul, who may or may not have been Peter III's son. (Catherine claimed in her memoirs that he was the son of Sergei Saltykov.) Catherine ruled for thirty-four years. She took on other lovers and remained on good terms with all of them when she grew tired of their attentions. Her last lover was Prince Platon Zubov, who was almost forty years her junior.

In 1796, Catherine suffered a stroke. She was nursed for several hours before she expired; she was said to have died from apoplexy. As for the story about her supposedly fatal equine encounter, it's only slightly less ridiculous than another rumor that circulated—that she died when the toilet she was sitting on collapsed due to her excessive weight.

Q How did "The Star-Spangled Banner" become the national anthem of the United States?

A As is the case with so many of the songs we know and love, "The Star-Spangled Banner" emerged from a fateful pairing of two potent forces: amateur poetry and alcohol.

On September 13, 1814, during the War of 1812, the British navy began a twenty-five-hour bombardment of Fort McHenry, Maryland, in an attempt to attack the city of Baltimore. A lawyer named Francis Scott Key witnessed the battle and, upon seeing the American flag raised in victory early the next morning, was moved to write a poem about it.

Just as you sometimes wake up in the morning with Debby Boone's "You Light Up My Life" inexplicably running through your head, Key had a tune rattling around in his noggin as the sun rose on September 14. It was "To Anacreon in Heaven," a popular British drinking song, and Key used its meter to guide his writing. The result was a four-stanza poem titled "The Defence of Fort McHenry." Key published the work almost immediately, along with instructions to sing the words to the tune of the drinking ditty. The poem was distributed throughout Baltimore. In October 1814, when it was published in sheet-music form, the song bore the more poignant title of "The Star-Spangled Banner."

The song steadily gained popularity throughout the nineteenth century, and by the time of the Civil War, it was a staple at patriotic events and had even been played at its first baseball game, at Brooklyn's Union Grounds Ballpark on May 15, 1862. By the 1890s, the song was a required component of military ceremonies, and in the early years of the twentieth century, the push began to make it the U.S. national anthem. After about twenty years and more than forty attempts at various bills and resolutions, Congress made "The Star-Spangled Banner" the national anthem on March 3, 1931. Before then, the national anthem was "My Country 'Tis of Thee."

It is customary to sing only the first of the song's four stanzas, which is probably just as well. A study done in 2005 revealed that 61 percent of Americans don't know all the words to even the first stanza. Furthermore, the second and third stanzas contain lyrics that are somewhat hostile to the British, and they're now our friends. During the Queen's next visit to the United States, it probably would be considered poor taste to sing that British "blood has wash'd out of their foul footstep's pollution."

Q Why is the bald eagle the U.S. national bird?

A After the U.S. founding fathers kicked the Brits out and hung up the "Under New Management" sign, they needed a few essential accessories: a system of government to run the joint, a flag to identify its ships, and a Great Seal for authenticating international treaties and agreements. Oddly enough, the Great Seal turned out to be a tricky one: Jefferson,

Franklin, Adams, and the gang started spit-balling ideas on July 4, 1776. During the next six years, three different committees pitched designs, but Congress rejected all of them. In 1782, Congress gave the three unsatisfactory proposals to the Secretary of the Continental Congress, Charles Thomson, and asked him to take a crack at it.

Thomson liked certain elements from each of the earlier attempts, including a small white eagle from the third committee. As a history and classics buff, he knew that eagles had a long history as national emblems. Roman soldiers carried eagle-topped staffs into battle; medieval knights slapped them on their family coats of arms; and Germany, Russia, and Poland adopted them as national symbols. But while he liked the iconic nobility and strength of the eagle, Thomson thought it was important that the U.S. symbol be something unique to America, to underscore the young nation's independence from Europe. So he changed the bird to the bald eagle, which is indigenous to North America. (Incidentally, "bald" doesn't have anything to do with hair loss in this case—the term dates back to the thirteenth century and describes white coloration on the head.)

After less than a week of brainstorming, Thomson gave his ideas to one of the more artistically inclined members of the earlier committees, who produced a polished drawing of the design. Exactly one week after being tasked with the Seal design, Thomson presented these drawings to the Continental Congress, along with his own written description of the Great Seal (called a blazon), with the bald eagle as the central figure. Congress approved the design the same day, and the Great Seal was a hit. Before long, the eagle took off as a national symbol, and it was everywhere: money, buildings, novelty butter churns—the works.

Not everyone was a fan, however. In a 1784 letter to his daughter, Benjamin Franklin dissed the bald eagle as "a bird of bad moral character," because of its habit of stealing fish from the fishing hawk. He suggested that the turkey would make a better choice, noting, "The turkey is in comparison a much more respectable bird... he is besides (though a little vain and silly, it is true, but not the worse emblem for that) a bird of courage, and would not hesitate to attack a grenadier of the British guards, who should presume to invade his farm yard with a red coat on."

Franklin wasn't entirely serious, of course, but who knows? If he had pitched the idea a few years earlier, we might be known as the fightin' turkeys.

Q Was there a real King Arthur?

A You've seen the movies: *Camelot, Excalibur, King Arthur*— even the Disney feature *The Sword in the Stone*. Is there truth behind the romantic myth of King Arthur? Of course. Can history prove that a good king named Arthur lived in England before, say, AD 1000? No.

Britain was part of the Roman Empire—perhaps an unwilling part—for nearly four centuries. In AD 410, though, Rome's control of the island shriveled and its armies withdrew. Chieftains and bands of lawless raiders fought for control. In the power vacuum that developed, an anti-Roman leader named Vortigern emerged to become king through acts of conspiracy and murder. A ruler with varying levels of reputation depending on the chronicler, Vortigern opened the door to Saxon mercenaries to help him repel Pict and Irish invaders. Ultimately, both the Saxons and the British turned on Vortigern, who burned to death in the castle in which he had taken refuge from his enemies.

A new leader rose to rally the many chieftains in England—a man named Ambrosius Aurelianus, who had led the British rebellion against Vortigern. Apparently born of a Roman or half-Roman family, Ambrosius imposed order in the countryside. He contained the Saxons and made the roads safe to travel. Peace settled on the land and trade flourished.

What does this have to do with Arthur? Ambrosius won the great Battle of Badon. Three accounts survive of this long-ago fight, and one of them credits a man named Arthur with victory. This account, written by the monk Nennius, who lived at least a hundred years later, says that at Badon, Arthur killed 960 men single-handedly, and that he won eleven other battles with the Saxons as well.

This seems to be the beginning of the legend. Many more years passed; Arthur the mighty warrior turned up in a few epics, legends, and poems from the British Isles. In the twelfth century, Geoffrey of Monmouth wrote the *History of the Kings of England*, in which Arthur is a mighty king with Guinevere at his side and Merlin serving as a prophet and advisor. How much of Geoffrey's work was based on histories and tales now lost? How much was his imagination? We do not know.

After Geoffrey, other writers, like Thomas Malory, embroidered what truth there was and turned it into marvelous, romantic fiction. Some of the stories of the Knights of the Round Table no doubt spring from older tales. The sword in the stone, for example, was an object worshipped a thousand years earlier by Sarmatian troops who were stationed in Britain by the Roman Empire.

The original Arthur probably did exist, but as a mighty war leader, not a king. The romance of Camelot, though, is wide open to interpretation. Since no one knows anything for sure, you can believe whatever you like.

Q Were there female druids?

A Absolutely. The Celts—the culture that produced druids— were far less gender-biased than their Greek and Roman neighbors. In Celtic societies, women could buy or inherit property, assume leadership, wage war, divorce men, and, yes, become druids.

Druids were the leaders—spiritually, intellectually, and sometimes politically—of the Celts. Because they did not use writing, we don't know exactly what druids (or their followers) believed or what they taught. From ancient stories, we've learned that they were well-educated and served as judges, scientists, teachers, priests, and doctors. Some even led their tribes.

At one time, Celtic tribes covered most of Europe, and their druids embodied wisdom and authority. In the ensuing centuries, however, druids have gotten a bad rap, due to lurid tales of human sacrifice that may or may not be true. Most of the bad-mouthing came from enemies of the Celts, so take what they said with the proverbial grain of salt.

Femme druids were described as priestesses, prophets, and oracles by Greek writers like Plutarch and Romans such as Tacitus. Several ancient authors mention holy women living on island sanctuaries, either alone or alongside male druids.

Irish tales are full of druids, some of them women. They helped win battles by transforming trees into warriors, they conjured up storms and diseases, and sometimes they hid children from murderous fathers. In the Irish epic *Cattle Raid of Cooley,* a beautiful young druid named Fidelma foretells victory for the hero Cúchulainn. Saint Patrick met female druids, and Saint Bridget, by some accounts the daughter of a druid, may have been a druid herself before converting to Christianity.

The ancient Celts knew what the rest of the world has slowly come to realize: Women can wield power as wisely—or as cruelly—as men.

Q What was World War I called before World War II?

A We certainly don't name wars like we used to. Once, we had poetry in our conflicts. We had the Pastry War, the War of the Roses, and the War of the Oranges. We had the War of the Three Sanchos, the War of the Three Henries, and the War of the Eight Saints. We even had something called the War of Jenkins' Ear.

As the twentieth century rolled around, this convention of applying sweet nicknames to war—and everything else—was still going strong. Ty Cobb was given the moniker "The Georgia Peach." And the 1904 World's Fair was not-so-humbly called "The Greatest of Expositions." It was an optimistic time. Advances in medicine were helping people live longer and Henry Ford's mass production of the automobile made the world seem smaller than ever.

This combination of optimism and the tradition of poetic nick-names led to some understandable debate in 1914, when an assassin's bullet felled the Archduke Franz Ferdinand and launched all of Europe—and much of the world—into all-out war. For the next few years, Germans rampaged through the continent, looking rather silly in spiked hats; mustard gas (which was not nearly as delicious as it sounded) crippled and killed countless men and women; and all across Europe, an entire generation was slowly wiped out.

What to name this gruesome conflict? The journalists and historians went to work. A number of possibilities were discarded, including "The German War" and "The War of the Nations," before two names were settled upon, which are still used today in conjunction with World War I: "The Great War," which retains a simplistic elegance, and, more popularly, "The War to End All Wars."

Melodramatic? Yes. Full of hubris? Definitely. Remember, though, these were the same people who famously labeled the Titanic "unsinkable."

No, we don't name wars like we used to. But even if the stylistic flourishes of yore have mostly disappeared, it is comforting to know that we're still not above a little hubris and melodrama. Anyone remember "Mission Accomplished"?

Q Whatever happened to Van Gogh's ear?

A Great artists are people of almost unfathomable passion. And from a recognized genius like Vincent van Gogh, you'd expect the sort of passion that rises to another level entirely. Throw said genius into a love triangle with friend and roommate Paul Gauguin and a trollop named Rachel, and you just know that someone was not going to make it out in one piece. In this instance, it was Van Gogh who came out on the losing end.

For Van Gogh, lopping off his own left earlobe has the distinction of being the artist's ultimate act of mental instability—overshadowing even his suicide. His self-mutilation has brought him unprecedented (if posthumous) attention. Most know the ear anecdote; some know that he did it for a woman. What has been lost to history is the final resting place of that little chunk of genius—whatever happened to the ear?

In December 1888, following an argument with Gauguin, who was also an artist, Van Gogh came at his friend with an open razor. Gauguin held him off. The content of the argument is likewise lost in the shadows of history; Van Gogh had been drinking absinthe almost nonstop, and he was prone to fits of violence and depression.

Back in his room, Van Gogh sliced off the lower portion of his left ear. He wrapped his severed lobe in a piece of cloth and walked to one of the many brothels he was known to frequent. Upon arrival, he requested a prostitute named Rachel. (Rumor has it that Van Gogh and Gauguin were in competition for this working girl's affections.) When she appeared at the door, he handed her what is easily one of the worst Christmas gifts of all time: a bloody piece of ear flesh. Rachel fainted. Feeling dejected, Van Gogh slumped back to his room and passed out. When Van Gogh was discovered by Gauguin and others, he exhibited only faint signs of life and was taken to a hospital.

This is where the ear passes out of the story. The artist checked himself in and out of a mental institution before taking his own life seven months later. Presumably, based on her, shall we say, unenthusiastic response to her beau's unique gift, Rachel discarded the ear upon returning to her senses. Since the only mention of Rachel in history books is a description of Van Gogh's short visit (said books do not even make mention of her last name), what she actually did with the ear remains a mystery.

Such is the sad fate of the artist: putting painstaking effort into a project, only to have the final product go unappreciated.

Q Who invented the car?

A The car as we know it today was invented by Karl Benz, who distilled centuries of accumulated wisdom, added a dose of original thinking, and unleashed upon the world the 1886 Benz Patent Motorwagen.

"Unleashed" is a strong word to describe the debut of a three-wheel contraption with nine-tenths of a horsepower and a top speed of 9.3 miles per hour. But the machine that trundled over the cobblestones of Mannheim, Germany, on July 3, 1886, was the first self-propelled vehicle to employ a gasoline-powered internal combustion engine as part of a purpose-built chassis—the basic definition of the modern automobile.

Something so momentous seldom occurs without a qualifier, however—and so it is with the Benz Patent Motorwagen.

For Karl Benz, the qualifier was another vehicle that first ran under its own power in 1886, just sixty miles away in Cannstatt, Germany. It was the inventive handiwork of partners Gottlieb Daimler and Wilhelm Maybach. Their machine also used a gas-burning single-cylinder engine, but it was mounted on a horse-type carriage. Daimler's carriage was specially constructed by a Stuttgart coachbuilder for this purpose, and had the four-wheel layout that eventually became standard practice.

But when forced to decide, historians give the edge to Benz as the "inventor" of the automobile. His patent was issued first (in January 1886); his Motorwagen was in operation at least a month before Daimler and Maybach's; and vitally, Benz's three-wheeler was not a horseless carriage but an entirely new type of vehicle, the marker for a new age of mobility.

Others quickly followed. The Duryea brothers, Charles and Frank, of Springfield, Massachusetts, put America on gas-powered wheels with their motorized carriage in September 1893. Henry Ford's first car, the experimental Quadracycle, sputtered to life in Detroit in June 1896.

By 1901, enough tinkerers had walked in the footsteps of Benz and Daimler that car building was a full-fledged industry. As for those two German pioneers, they never met face to face, but the rival companies they formed became tightly laced. Daimler proved to be the more successful carmaker. He was quicker to develop his machines, and they entranced a wealthy and colorful Austrian named Emil Jellinek. Jellinek placed large orders for Daimler automobiles, became a member of the company's board, and wielded enough influence to insist that its cars be named for his ten-year-old daughter, Mercedes.

Weathering tough times after World War I, the Daimler and Benz companies formed a syndicate to market their products, and when they merged in 1926, they created a company that combined the names of their autos, which honored the inventor of the car, along with the daughter of Emil Jellinek: Mercedes-Benz.

Q Why does the Leaning Tower of Pisa lean?

A To understand why the tower leans, one should know the history of this remarkable crooked erection, including where it was built. At the turn of the first century AD, Pisa was a vibrant seaport city on the northwestern coast of Italy. In 1063, the Pisans attacked the city of Palermo. (And yes, this is where the phrase "Hey, Pisan!" comes from.) They were victorious and returned home with treasures.

The Pisans, being a proud people, wanted to show the world how important their city was, and decided to erect a great cathedral complex, called the Field of Miracles; the complex included a cathedral, cemetery, baptistery, and bell tower.

Pisa was originally named Poseidonia in 600 BC, from a Greek word meaning "marshy land." Bonanno Pisano, the original architect of the bell tower, did not think this was important information when he began the project. In 1173, Bonanno decided that since there was a good deal of water under the ground, he'd build a shallow foundation, one that was about three meters deep.

Five years later, when third-floor construction was about to begin, Bonanno realized that his structure was sinking on one side; this was because he built upon a bed of dense clay. But being a proud Pisan, he continued to go skyward. To attempt to solve the problem, he added two inches to the southern columns and thought no one would notice. People noticed. The third floor reached completion, and the job was halted indefinitely.

In 1272, construction of the bell tower resumed under the guidance of architect Giovanni di Simone. He completed four more floors, built at an angle to compensate for the listing. But not only did his remedy cause the tower to tilt in the other direction, but it also created a curve. In 1284, the job was once again halted. In 1319, the Pisans picked up their tools and completed the seventh floor. The bell tower was added in 1372, and then it was left to lean in peace until the nineteenth century.

In 1838, the foundation was dug out so visitors could see how it was built, which caused the tower to lean even more Then in 1934, Benito Mussolini ordered the foundation to be reinforced with concrete. The concrete was too heavy, however, and it sunk the tower further into the clay.

Since then, many projects have come and gone; the tower is now stabilized and was reopened in 2001, so tourists can walk to the top. The Leaning Tower of Pisa is the top tourist attraction in Tuscany. The circular tower stands nearly 185 feet tall, is estimated to weigh almost sixteen thousand tons, has a 294-step spiral staircase, and leans at an angle of almost four degrees, meaning that the tower is about four meters off vertical. And to top it off, researchers from the University of Pisa found the tower to be sinking at a rate of one-twentieth of an inch annually. At that rate, they've predicted, the tower will collapse in fewer than three hundred years.

Q Why were fashion styles so ugly in the 1970s?

A Ironically, it boils down to two hugely contradictory forces: anti-establishment protest and the military/industrial complex. When you have a union this unholy, polyester bell-bottoms and grotesque flower-print shirts are the inevitable result.

Let's start with the protest part. When the mid-1960s rolled around, after America's idealism had been shattered by the Vietnam War and the death of John F. Kennedy, there were tremendous shifts in societal perceptions. Traditional notions of race, class, and culture were suddenly under assault, fueled in great part by young people asserting their feelings in ways that were unlike any American generation before them. They brazenly rebelled against their parents' notions of work, family, moral values, music, education, and more.

And they dressed like it, because in all humans who have a choice of what to wear, there is a natural inclination to let clothes express your sense of self and your place in the world. Protesting kids in the late 1960s and early 1970s dressed in ways that were outwardly outlandish, but nevertheless seemed attractive because they represented exciting, cutting-edge, and important new views of the world.

Their dads had worn short hair, so the young men of this generation wore theirs long. Their parents had worn conservatively cut and traditionally colored clothes made from natural fabrics like cotton and wool, so they wore Technicolor hues and exaggerated shapes, like elephant bell-bottoms and floppy collars.

This is not to say it was just the kids—stylish parents took to some of these innovations, too, though perhaps not as outrageously. But all in all, society was taken with stretching the boundaries, trying new things, and expressing itself in new, less-constrained ways. A certain outlandishness persisted through the late 1970s and the disco era. Then, fashion made a sharp return to conservatism, embodied in the "preppy" clothing movement of the late 1970s, which wrenched clothing back to more classic lines and natural fabrics. The more straitlaced era was reflected in the culture as well, with the election of Ronald Reagan in 1980.

But what of the military/industrial complex? Artificial fabrics like polyester—which were staples of the 1970s and allowed many of the flamboyant styles to be even more so—were an outgrowth of a kind of scientific utopianism that characterized the United States after World War II. The decades after the war saw stunning technological breakthroughs in every area and fostered a belief that science could solve any human problem. (We're still waiting, however, for Richard Nixon's War on Cancer to be declared a victory.)

The combination of national prosperity and a technology sector that carried great momentum from the war resulted in "advances" like polyester, which was invented during the war and was parlayed into countless uses thereafter. So while hippies and disco divas thought they were thumbing their noses at conventional culture, they were clad in one of its offspring: yucky polyester. Oh, the irony!

Q Why do judges wear black robes?

A Because black is slimming, of course!

If only it were that easy. The real reason judges wear black robes is up for debate, though only slightly. Ask any member of the Catholic Church and he or she will tell you that this practice is purely an ecclesiastical tradition. During the fifteen hundreds, priests wore black robes. And during this time, priests were—you guessed it—judges, too.

But black wasn't the end-all back then. English court dress was quite flamboyant, to say the least. Judges would wear a black robe trimmed in fur during the winter months and a violet or scarlet robe trimmed in pink taffeta during the summer months. No wonder these robes were referred to as "costumes" in the Judges' Rules that were set forth after 1635. Judges also wore black girdles underneath their robes.

Court dress continued to evolve, and accessories were piled onto the already ornate ensemble. By the mid-eighteenth century, judges began to take even more liberties with their costumes. For criminal trials, they wore scarlet robes with a matching hood and a black scarf. For civil trials, many judges kept it simple and wore a black silk gown. After years and years of indecisiveness and plenty of lilac and mauve, most courts settled on the simple black silk gown as a base. Ceremonial occasions were (and still are) an entirely different beast—we're talking silk stockings, leather pumps, and all kinds of shiny buckles. But that's a different story.

Today, the black robe is fairly standard in courtrooms around the world (depending on the court or level). In the good old USA, the black robe is definitely the garb of choice. You will never see a U.S. judge (in open court) decked out in fur trim, bright colors (definitely not pink), and, um, a girdle.

While the Catholics' explanation of why judges wear black robes makes the most sense, there are other explanations to consider: Black symbolizes a lack of favor to one side or another, and black is appropriate in a criminal trial because of the dark nature of the proceedings.

In the end, it boils down to this: The majority of judges feel that wearing a black robe during court proceedings is an unwritten rule. With the exception of the United States Solicitor General— who is usually dressed in late-nineteenth-century attire (morning coat, gray ascot, vest, and pinstriped pants)—and the judges of the Maryland Court of Appeals—who wear scarlet robes—it is rare to see a U.S. judge in any color other than black.

Chapter Nine

HEALTH MATTERS

Q Why does sugar rot your teeth?

A Remember the old commercial in which four out of five dentists recommended Trident chewing gum? You may not have realized it then, but Trident was the world's first sugarless gum—and we all know that dentists hate sugar, because it causes tooth decay.

But what exactly is so corrosive about sugar? It starts with plaque. All of us, no matter how hard we brush, have plaque on our teeth. That's why it's so important to go to the dentist twice a year for the brutal scraping that removes the buildup of plaque. Plaque is kind of fascinating—in a disgusting way—because it is composed of millions of different kinds of bacteria that come together to form the translucent film on your teeth.

Your mouth isn't exactly the cleanest place, and bacteria love to feast on the same foods that you do—especially sugar. In fact, eating sugar is like dumping gasoline onto the inferno of bacteria that is already raging inside your mouth.

It turns out that bacteria process sugar much like people do. If you've ever gotten a jittery rush from eating a candy bar, you know that sugar can be converted into energy quite quickly. Bacteria react in the same manic way, though there's a corrosive twist. When bacteria (or any organism, for that matter) break down sugar into energy, the by-product is several types of acid, including lactic acid. This process is known as glycolysis. Lactic acid, when built up over time, can start to eat away at the calcium phosphate in your tooth enamel; this is the beginning of a cavity.

So don't be deceived by sugar. There's nothing sweet about it.

Q What's the trick to breastfeeding triplets?

A This one boils down to the age-old tension between supply and demand. Can a new mother produce enough breast milk to satisfy the demands of three infants? Putting aside for a moment the massive logistical constraints of breastfeeding triplets, the answer is a resounding "Yes." After all, dogs have been known to nurse way more than three puppies at one time.

Not that we want to compare women to female dogs, but...
okay, let's just move on.

The process of breastfeeding is one of many miracles related to
childbirth. Whether a woman has two, three, or six children, her
body is programmed to produce enough milk to feed all of her
offspring.

When a woman breastfeeds,
two hormones are released in
her body: prolactin and oxytocin.
The sensation of a baby nursing stimulates nerves in the areola, which
instruct the pituitary gland to
produce more prolactin, the
hormone that stimulates the
production of milk. Oxytocin
causes the muscles around the
cells that produce milk to contract, "letting down" the milk so
the baby can access it. With a steady supply of these hormones, a
mother can nurse multiple babies for as long as she sees fit.

Now, if it's the logistics of breastfeeding triplets that you're wondering about—well, it requires some deft maneuvering. Naturally,
the babies have to take turns, and some mothers may prefer to
give one baby a bottle of formula per feeding to cut down on
chaffing and irritation.

La Leche League International, an organization that offers advice
on nursing, says it's quite possible to put both breasts to work
simultaneously. It's merely a matter of using multiple pillows to
support the weight of the two babies. Imagine if women had a
third breast. Nursing triplets would really be a snap.

Q Why do women live longer than men?

A Perhaps wearing pink somehow extends the life of a lady. Or maybe sugar, spice, and everything nice are better for the heart and mind than snips, snails, and puppy dog tails. Those poor, tailless puppy dogs—it must be karma.

Women ages one hundred and older outnumber men nine to one (good news for centenarian single men), and women sixty-five and older outnumber men three to two. Biology is a large factor when it comes to living to such a ripe old age. Because women have always been the primary caregivers for their offspring, they have more evolutionary reason to live long: They need to stick around to raise their children and grandchildren. This evolutionary drive may have helped women develop greater resistance than men to heart disease and other leading killers.

Behavior is a factor, too. Between the ages of fifteen and twenty-four, men are far more likely to die than women (around four to five times more likely, in fact). This is the age when testosterone brings about more reckless and risky behavior in men. Like the red male cardinal or the peacock, human men are wired to get the attention of female partners, and an abundance of testosterone helps get the job done.

Humans in the modern age have many more opportunities for risky behavior than our ancestors did, so sometimes that testosterone encourages behavior that has nothing to do with its original purpose. In general, throughout their lives men take more risks when driving, consume more alcohol, take more drugs, and smoke more cigarettes than women. Unintentional injuries were the fifth-leading cause of death for American men in 2005, according to the Centers for Disease Control and Prevention. More than twice as many men die in car accidents as women.

So, dudes, buckle your seatbelts, buy some nicotine gum, pick a good day to stop sniffing glue, and try to use only one side of your beer helmet. Then maybe we can all get old together and hate on the youth culture.

Q Can popping a zit kill you?

A The death-by-zit-popping stories that made their way through the halls in high school weren't urban legends after all. Popping a zit really can cause a grave infection.

While it may be exceedingly tempting to free yourself of an impacted patch of skin, it's not wise to squeeze away unless you've paid utmost attention to sanitation and sterilization. Bacteria exist on skin, as well as on your fingernails. Popping a zit can spread these bacteria around and push them deeper into hazardous territory.

The face is an especially vulnerable place to acquire an infection because this is where the sinus cavity and vital blood vessels to the brain are located. This danger zone, known to the medical and dental community as the Danger Triangle of the Face, starts at the bridge of the nose and fans out toward the corners of the mouth. Inside the skull, behind the eye sockets, sits a cavernous sinus at the base of the brain. This collection of large veins drains deoxygenated blood from the brain and face back to the heart.

If careless pimple-picking flares into an infection, it could set off a local tissue inflammation called cellulitis, which could spread to the cavernous sinus. Cavernous sinus thrombosis (CST) could then occur, wherein the blood in the sinus forms an infected clot and blocks a large vein at the base of the brain. Although CST is rare, it is potentially fatal. Treatment options include antibiotics and surgical drainage.

CST isn't the only worry for zit-poppers. If a person has a weakened immune system, a rupture in the skin can serve as an entryway for a range of other serious complications, including severe strains of staph infections such as toxic shock syndrome (TSS) and methicillin-resistant *Staphylococcus aureus* (MRSA, a drug-resistant staph).

Caused by staph bacteria, which one-third of humans hold on the surface of their skin, TSS can move rapidly. In a matter of a few days or even hours, blood pressure can drop dangerously and circulation can be cut off to the extremities as the body diverts blood to vital organs. In extreme cases, gangrene can develop in the fingers and toes.

MRSA is graver still, carrying life-threatening infections to bones, joints, surgical wounds, the bloodstream, heart valves, and lungs. As with CST, antibiotics and surgical drainage are the weapons used to fight TSS and MRSA. (A handful of medications, such as vancomycin, do work against MRSA.)

Bet you didn't know a little ol' zit could cause such big trouble. The lesson? Use prudence when you pop that pimple. Better yet, don't pop it at all. The result could be more dire than you ever imagined.

Q Why do they sterilize the needle before a lethal injection?

A The United States is a nation terrified of germs. Inundated by media reports of flu pandemics, new strains of drug-resistant tuberculosis, untreatable "superbugs," and mysterious flesh-eating bacteria, Americans put paper on toilet seats, push disinfected carts at the grocery store, and buy millions of dollars worth of antibacterial hand gel each year. Americans also, for some reason, sterilize needles before lethally injecting condemned prisoners. Seems a little overboard, doesn't it?

Actually, there are many reasons for the use of sterilized needles in lethal injections, the most obvious being to protect the lethal injector. A slip of the hand, an inadvertent twitch, a poorly timed sneeze—one can imagine a number of scenarios in which the needle might go astray.

Indeed, the history of capital punishment in the United States is littered with bungled executions that would be amusing if they weren't so disturbing. Poison gas has been improperly administered, needles have shot from veins mid-injection, and in more than once case, the heads of electrocuted inmates have burst into flames. By far the largest number of botched executions has come via lethal injection, though usually the biggest problem is finding a suitable vein to insert the needle (as a number of death-row inmates are habitual drug users).

A second reason for sterilization is the rare possibility (though perhaps less rare now, in the age of DNA evidence) that the criminal could be exonerated or earn a stay of execution at the very last moment—perhaps even after the needle has been inserted.

We can hear you now: "Oh, come on! That would never happen!" *Au contraire.* Consider the case of James Autry, convicted of the April 1980 murder of two people at a convenience store in Texas. In October 1983, Autry's turn on the lethal injection gurney (doesn't quite have the same grim ring as the electric chair, does it?) finally came. He was strapped down, the IV inserted into his vein. Onlookers leaned forward in anticipation. Suddenly, just as the sodium thiopental was about to be administered, the proceedings were interrupted with word that Autry had been granted a stay of execution by a Supreme Court judge, and Autry was unhooked.

Sounds like the stuff of Hollywood, doesn't it? Not really. In March 1984, Autry was executed anyway. It was Texas, after all.

Q How does soap get us clean?

A You've been out working in the garden all day, getting down and dirty. Now it's time for a little wood ash and animal fat to get yourself clean. Jump in the shower, add some salt and vegetable oil to the mix, and you should be feeling fresh as a daisy.

Doesn't sound too promising, huh?

Well, it wouldn't be if you dumped all of the above over your head at once, but fortunately someone has already combined them into one easy-to-use package. It's called soap. Wood ash, fat, salt, and oil are the essential ingredients of soap. Every bar contains them (or their chemical equivalents), whether you got it for $0.99 at a drugstore or $9.99 at an exclusive boutique.

In soap making, wood ash is boiled down in water to create a caustic solution otherwise known as lye. Under normal circumstances, lye is definitely not something you would want anywhere near your skin. But when you add fat, a mysterious transformation called *saponification* takes place. Basically, this means the lye and fat molecules join to create a single long molecule consisting of oxygen, carbon, hydrogen, and sodium. If you want to get all scientific, it's written like this: $CH_3\text{-}(CH_2)_n\text{-}CONa$.

Now this molecule can perform a pretty nifty trick. The fatty carbon-hydrogen end you see on the far left gloms on to a tiny particle of grease or dirt on your skin. The sodium at the opposite end attaches itself to a water molecule, and whoosh—the grime slides off. In other words, a soap molecule is like a tiny chain with a hook for dirt at one end and water at the other.

Who were the first people to figure this out? Archaeologists have discovered evidence of soap making in the Near East going back to around 2800 BC. One possible theory is that the ashes of wood fires would become saturated with the fat of roasting animals. If it happened to rain before the ashes cooled, the ashes would start bubbling up in an interesting way. Eventually women discovered this strange bubbly stuff was good for scrubbing pots, garments, and the occasional squalling kid, too. Soap was born.

If you're worried about too many trees being sacrificed for cleanliness, rest assured that soap today is made largely from caustic soda produced artificially in a laboratory. And if you're a vegetarian, there are plenty of animal-free soaps to choose from. The idea behind their manufacture still remains the same, however. So grab a bar, thank your ancestors for this humble invention, and get yourself squeaky clean!

Q How fast are you going when you're running amok?

A It's difficult to calculate how fast your head can spin when you're rushing around in such a frenzy. You had better take a chill pill, dude. After all, you don't want to be diagnosed with amok. It's an actual psychiatric condition, which might surprise you since it's used so casually in conversation.

In eighteenth-century Southeast Asia (where the term originated), however, there was nothing casual about it. Studying the etymology of amok, we find the word had its origins in the Malay *mengamok*, which means to make a desperate and furious charge. The term was originally used as a noun, and it was meant to denote a Malay tribesman in the midst of a homicidal rage.

Unfortunately, this was somewhat of a common cultural occurrence over there. According to Malay mythology, running amok occurred when the evil tiger spirit (known as the *hantu belian*) entered a person's body and caused him or her to act violently, without conscious awareness.

British explorer Captain James Cook documented his own observations of Malays running amok during his travels to that part of the world in 1770. His records describe frenzied individuals killing and maiming villagers and animals indiscriminately and without apparent cause.

Amok was first classified as a psychiatric illness around 1849, and it's no longer a rare anthropological curiosity confined to primitive Malaysian culture. In modern society, the term (though antiquated) can still be used to describe a mentally unstable individual's homicidal behavior that results in multiple fatalities and injuries.

However, in everyday conversation, running amok is more commonly—and more lightheartedly—synonymous with "going crazy," "going postal," or just "raising hell." And that's in the colloquial and nonviolent sense, thank goodness.

Q Is it still possible to contract the Black Death?

A The Black Death is alive and well. But as long as the human population continues to feel that it would rather not willingly share its space with thousands of rats, most people's bodies should remain refreshingly plague-free.

The Black Death killed twenty-five million Europeans from 1347 to 1353, or one-third of the continent's population. The plague is caused by the bacteria *Yersinia pestis*, which mainly spreads when a flea bites an infected rat (or other rodent) for breakfast and then bites a human for lunch or dinner, thus passing on the bacteria. The plague comes in three flavors: bubonic, pneumonic, and septicemic.

Bubonic is the cover girl of the bunch—the one most people associate with the term "plague." The telltale symptom of bubonic plague is buboes, infected lymph notes on the neck, armpit, and groin. They turn black and ooze blood and puss.

Pneumonic plague occurs when a person inhales the bacteria from someone who is infected. "Cover your mouth when you sneeze," has never made more sense than with this little ditty.

Septicemic plague is when *Yersinia pestis* gets into your bloodstream. It can cause gangrene due to tissue death in extremities like fingers and toes, turning them black. The gangrene and the black buboes and lesions all contributed to the term "Black Death."

Pneumonic and septicemic plague make bubonic plague look like a ray of hope: Untreated, they have close to a 100 percent mortality rate. Bubonic's death rate is a measly 60 to 75 percent if left untreated.

The fact that most people live in much more sanitary conditions these days means that the chances of getting the plague are low. However, it is still very much around. In India, between August and October 1994, 693 people contracted the plague, and fifty-six of them died. Ten to fifteen cases are reported every year in the United States, and there are one thousand to three thousand annual cases globally. Animals that carry the plague are found in Asia, Africa, and North and South America. Additionally, plague is a perfect candidate for biological warfare, particularly pneumonic plague since it can be airborne.

Treatment includes a very aggressive dose of antibiotics, which must begin early to improve the chance of survival. The Centers for Disease Control and Prevention recommends that people traveling in rural places that might harbor the disease take precautions against it. Those with the highest risk should start on preemptive antibiotics. Others should use insect repellent on their bodies and clothing.

So, if you're traveling in an area where you could be bitten by a plague-carrying flea, try to stick to bed-and-breakfasts run by human beings and skip the rodent-owned ones. Nothing ruins a vacation like the Black Death.

Q Are fat people or skinny people more likely to die in a car crash?

A A spare tire in your trunk is a good thing if you have a blowout. Turns out, a spare tire around your waist is a bad thing if you have a car accident.

Heavier people are more than twice as likely as skinnier people to be killed or seriously injured in a car crash—and the primary reason may surprise you. Experts analyzed thousands of road accidents from 1993 to 2004 and found the fatality rate to be 2.25 times higher for the morbidly obese than for the less hefty.

How an overweight body reacts in a collision plays a role in crashes—more on that in a moment—but the main reason the corpulent die more in car accidents is that they aren't as likely to be wearing a seatbelt. It seems the seriously stout find it a big fat pain to belt up. Merely reaching for the belt, pulling it across, and locating the latch is a chore for the chunky, researchers found.

Wearing a seatbelt is the biggest safety advantage in an accident, reducing your chances of dying by 60 percent and of being seriously injured by 65 percent. According to a study done by Vanderbilt University, only 83 percent of the driving population as a whole wears a seatbelt, and just 70 percent of obese Americans do. The figure drops to barely 55 percent of the morbidly obese. (These terms are defined by the National Institutes of Health Body Mass Index, a sliding scale based on height and weight. It says, for example, that a five-foot, seven-inch adult is obese at 191 pounds and morbidly obese at 255. A five-foot, ten-inch adult is obese starting at 209 pounds, morbidly obese at 278.)

The problem is spreading. The National Highway Traffic Safety Agency says that thirty-eight million Americans (19 percent of the population) have a girth that exceeds the seatbelt length required by law. And it's worth noting that most automakers today install belts eighteen to twenty inches longer than specified by federal law; in the mid-1990s, it was twelve inches longer than required. Easier access to seatbelt extensions, restraints that fit more comfortably, and greater promotion of seatbelt use are among ideas aimed at addressing the avoirdupois.

Researchers do cite some less significant fat-related factors behind the kill rate: It's not easy to extricate the porcine from a crumpled car, accidents can trigger a variety of weight-induced health problems, and heavier people bring more harmful mass to the impact when collision forces fling them into the dashboard or windshield.

On a positive note, fat people who survive crashes tend to suffer fewer abdominal injuries than skinny people because they have more natural padding. Thanks, spare tire!

Q What is mistletoe good for besides a Christmas kiss?

A First off, Christmas kisses are nothing to sneer at. When else do you get to grab and snog complete strangers because a plant sprig happens to be hanging from a well-placed nail?

That custom, by the way, is loosely based upon a Norse myth in which Frigga, goddess of love, restores her son to life and joyfully kisses everyone in sight. Combined with a bit of Victorian romanticism, kissing under the mistletoe became a popular pastime. But what's so special about mistletoe?

The plant has several unique traits that imbue it with meaning. First, it grows fruit and flourishes in the coldest months of the year, making it a symbol of fertility and life. Second, European mistletoe has paired leaves, and the berries exude sticky white juice, conveying certain sexual allusions. Third, it's a plant without roots that never touches the ground, giving it a mystical aura.

American mistletoe is toxic, while the European variety can be used medicinally. Europe's mistletoe, *Viscum album*, is found in herbal teas and shampoos. It has potential as a cancer treatment, and some study groups are actually conducting clinical trials with mistletoe lectins. Traditionally, *Viscum*

216 · Does Size Matter?

album was used by the Greeks, Celts, and other ancient folks to treat epilepsy and infertility, among other ills. It was also considered just plain lucky.

If you get your mistletoe in North America, though, be careful! Deer and certain birds eat the berries, but they are poisonous to humans. The American mistletoe seen at Christmas is called *Phoradendron*. At least thirteen hundred species of the plant exist, and many will do nasty things to your insides. While it makes a pretty holiday decoration, the plant is a parasitic pest that attaches itself to hardwood and fir trunks, digs in, and sucks water and sap from the host tree to stay alive.

Kinda like your ex-boyfriend or ex-girlfriend, huh? Grabbing a total stranger for a smooch next December may not be such a bad idea.

Chapter Ten

EARTH AND SPACE

Q Does anything live in the Dead Sea?

A The Red Sea isn't really red, and the Black Sea isn't really black—so what are the odds that the Dead Sea is really dead? Then again, if you've ever gone for a dip in the Dead Sea, you'll know that there is at least a shred of truth to the name. The Dead Sea's otherworldly qualities make swimmers buoyant— everyone's doing the "dead man's float."

Located between Israel and Jordan, the Dead Sea is, at thirteen hundred feet below sea level, the lowest surface point on Earth. The very bottom is twenty-three hundred feet below sea level. Water flows into the Dead Sea from the Jordan River, but then it has no place to go, since it's already reached the lowest possible surface point on the planet. The fresh water that flows into the Dead Sea evaporates quickly because of the high temperatures in the desert, and it leaves behind a deposit of minerals.

These minerals have accumulated to make the Dead Sea the pungent stew that it is today. Slightly more than 30 percent of the Dead Sea is comprised of minerals, including sodium chloride, iodine, calcium, potassium, and sulfur. These minerals have been marketed as therapeutic healing products for people with skin conditions; many cosmetic companies have their own line of Dead Sea products.

The Dead Sea is reported to be six times saltier than an ocean, and salt provides buoyancy for swimmers. No form of life could survive in these conditions, right? Not exactly. It's true that every species of fish introduced into this body of water has promptly died, but in 1936, an Israeli scientist found that microscopic pieces of green algae and a few types of bacteria were living in the Dead Sea. So the Dead Sea can't technically be considered dead.

At any rate, it's too late to change the Dead Sea's name—and that's probably just as well. Would the *Living Sea Scrolls* hold the same intrigue?

Q Why do tornadoes always seem to hit trailer parks?

A After a vicious tornado, there always seems to be a news report from a trailer park that has been reduced to a pile of crumpled aluminum and soiled NASCAR memorabilia. And it's just not fair because—let's face it—if you're hanging a store-bought "Bless This Mess" sign inside your doublewide, you've probably already rolled snake eyes in the game of life. Must the good Lord add insult to injury by making these homes on wheels a magnet for extreme weather? The answer is, he doesn't.

Tornadoes are just as inclined to hit a regular home as a mobile home, but the difference is that we are less likely to hear about it. The incidence of damage and fatalities from a tornado is much lower for regularly framed houses than it is for trailers. Unlike most houses, trailers are not secured with a sturdy concrete foundation; consequently, they have a better chance of breaking apart when subjected to a tornado's violent winds. To make matters worse, the objects from these broken-apart mobile homes become missiles that can take out the bunched-together residents. For example, if you are unlucky enough to get tagged by a novelty Confederate flag traveling at two hundred and fifty miles per hour, the South most certainly will not rise again.

So it's not that tornadoes are more likely to hit a trailer park—it's just that you are about twenty times more likely to die if you are in a mobile home during a tornado. Not even the Red Cross seems sure what to tell you if you're inside one of these relatively flimsy abodes when a storm is looming, stating the obvious with hints such as this: Watch the weather report, and leave your mobile home before the tornado hits!

And even if you somehow survive the tornado, your trailer is still more vulnerable to fires, floods, and just about any other destructive force than a house. It's starting to look like living in one of these things isn't such a good idea. By comparison, can moving back in with your parents really be that bad?

Q Are we going to be hit by a meteor?

A We already have been, and we will be again.

NASA estimates that about once every hundred years, a rocky asteroid or an iron meteorite substantial enough in size to cause tidal waves hits Earth's surface. About once every few hundred thousand years, an object strikes that is large enough to cause a global catastrophe.

NASA's Near Earth Objects program scans the skies and observes comets and asteroids that could potentially enter Earth's neighborhood. It has been keeping close tabs on an asteroid called Apophis, a.k.a. MN2004. According to NASA, on April 13, 2029, Apophis will be close enough to Earth that it will be visible to the naked eye. At one time, the odds were estimated to be as great as one in three hundred that Apophis would hit Earth. However, NASA has now ruled out a collision, which is a good thing be-

cause the asteroid would have hit Earth with the force of an 880-megaton explosion (more than fifty thousand times the power of the atomic bomb dropped on Hiroshima, Japan, in 1945).

Perhaps the best-known meteor hit occurred fifty thousand years ago, when an iron meteorite collided with what is now northern Arizona with a force estimated to be two thousand times greater than the bomb dropped on Hiroshima. Now named the Meteor Crater, the twelve-thousand-meters-wide crater is a popular tourist attraction.

A direct meteor hit isn't even necessary to cause significant damage. On June 30, 1908, what many believe was a small asteroid exploded high in the air near the Tunguska River in Russia. Taking into consideration the topography of the area, the health of the adjoining forest, and some new models concerning the dynamics of the explosion, scientists now believe that the force of the explosion was about three to five megatons. Trees were knocked down for hundreds of square miles.

NASA hopes to provide a few years' warning if there is a meteor approaching that could cause a global catastrophe. The organization anticipates that our existing technology would allow us to, among other things, set off nuclear fusion weapons near an object in order to deflect its trajectory. Or we can simply hope that Bruce Willis will save us, just like he did in the 1998 movie *Armageddon*.

Q Is the moon really made of green cheese?

A The notion that the moon is made of green cheese is less a myth than a rumor that never quite got a foothold in society. When it comes up in conversation, it's usually in a tongue-in-cheek sort of way, rather than as a serious discussion. There may be some people who believe the moon is indeed made of cheese—they're probably the same folks who would agree to put a down payment on the London Bridge.

Saying "the moon is made of green cheese" is roughly equivalent to saying the word "gullible" is not in the dictionary. The phrase began as an innocuous line in John Heywood's *Proverbes*, which was printed in 1546. It was utilized by writers of the period as an ironic and colorful way of saying a person would believe anything—no matter how blatantly false it might be. In its original context, "green" referred not to the color of the supposed cheese, but to its age. To say something is green is to say it is young and unripe.

More than 460 years later, the phrase has many colloquial uses. It is often substituted, for the purpose of illustration in philosophical arguments, for any statement known to the general public as false. Individuals now proudly claim that the moon is made of cheese, albeit facetiously, as evidence of their willingness to support an unpopular belief. And, of course, it is still used as a sarcastic be-all-end-all in a debate, a classic and comical way of saying a person is simple-minded: "If you believe [insert contested belief here], you probably believe the moon is made of cheese."

NASA appears to enjoy perpetuating the green cheese rumor. On April Fools' Day in 2002, the space-travel agency published a satellite photo of the moon that "proved" its make-up to be dairy. (The image showed an expiration date printed inside one of the moon's many craters.)

No word on whether someone tried to take a bite out of a moon rock.

Q Does plastic ever decompose?

A Those tree-hugging environmentalists are always trying to make you feel bad about carrying your groceries home in plastic bags. "Plastic takes five hundred years to decompose," they say. But really, how do they know? Plastics weren't invented until the twentieth century. It's not like Copernicus toted his astronomy books around in a plastic bag that is now blowing in the wind somewhere in Poland.

First, it's important to understand that there are many different types of plastic. Plastics are made from petroleum and other fossil fuels, and can be manufactured to various strengths and resistances to hot and cold. For instance, polythene is the type of plastic used to make children's toys, food packaging, and plastic shopping bags; it's not particularly strong. At the other end of the spectrum are epoxies, which are used, among other things, to make airplanes, including Harrier jets. Naturally, the stronger, more durable plastics take longer to decompose.

Let's stick with plastic shopping bags, a main eco-offender cited by environmentalists. In fairness, the claims of five hundred or even one thousand years are not completely unfounded. Bacteria and other microorganisms cannot feast on plastic bags the way they do on, say, banana peels because they do not recognize the manufactured substance as food. As a result, plastic bags do not biodegrade.

Plastic bags will, however, photodegrade. The ultraviolet light of the sun will eventually break a plastic bag down into smaller and smaller pieces, until it finally disappears. With direct sunlight, this process can be as short as ten to twenty years, not five hundred. The problem is, most plastic bags end up in landfills, where they are soon buried under other trash, and receive little or no sunlight. Suddenly, a thousand years seems a bit more plausible.

Do the environmentalists win this argument? Not so fast. Engineers have developed a way to make plastics out of starches found in corn and potatoes. Not only are these plastic bags more environmentally friendly to produce, but they also can break down in as little as ten days to a month if they are composted correctly—they contain 100 percent cornstarch, with vegetable oil for elasticity. Companies, including Wal-Mart, are switching to these bags, and they soon should be the accepted standard. Whatever the type of plastic—flimsy, durable, or corn-made—it will decompose. It's just a question of when.

Q Is it really darkest before the dawn?

A Someone once said: "It's always darkest before the dawn. So if you're going to steal the neighbor's newspaper, that's the time to do it."

If we're talking about metaphors and not about stealing newspapers, it does appear darkest just before the dawn. That is to say, a bad situation often seems worst right before it gets better. English dramatist John Webster conveyed this notion in his tragic 1614 play *The Duchess of Malfi*. In Act IV, Bosola says to the Duchess: "Leave this vain sorrow. Things being at the worst, begin to mend."

As a proverb, "It's always darkest before the dawn" has been around for centuries in various incarnations. Original credit usually goes to seventeenth-century British scholar and preacher Thomas Fuller. In *A Pisgah-Sight of Palestine* (1650), he wrote: "It is always darkest just before the day dawneth."

Today the old saying is still used in reference to just about every type of bad situation, from war to our own personal lives. Is it any wonder, then, that the phrase has inspired so many country crooners? Dwight Yoakam, Emmylou Harris, Dave Evans, and the Stanley Brothers have all recorded renditions of a song called "The Darkest Hour Is Just Before Dawn." So if you're feeling as brokenhearted, dejected, and bereft as a Nashville lover scorned, this could be the tune to add to your collection.

However, when you've run out of tissues and you're ready to look at this issue from a purely unemotional and scientific point of view, no, it is not literally darkest just before the dawn. The best time to don those night-vision goggles and swipe your neighbor's paper? Figure somewhere around mid-night—not 12:00 AM, but the actual halfway point between sunset and sunrise. Of course, that doesn't account for factors like glowing full moons and very bright streetlamps, so be sure to wear a ski mask.

Q Is there really such a thing as noise pollution?

A There certainly is, but this is a good question because it forces us to understand what the word "pollution" means. Most people know about pollution, thanks to government crusades to make us more aware of it and because, well, it's everywhere—in our surroundings, in our eyes, and in our lungs.

When we think of pollution, we tend to think of scattered trash, dirty air, or dangerous industrial chemicals that we don't see but learn about from news stories and political stumping. To understand noise pollution, we need to take a wider view of the word "pollution."

To define pollution as an "undesirable state of the natural environment being contaminated with harmful substances as a consequence of human activities," as *WordNet* does, doesn't quite get at noise pollution, because noise isn't a substance—it's simply the movement of air. But defining pollution as an "undesirable change in the physical, chemical or biological characteristics of the air, water or land that can harmfully affect the health, survival or activities of human or other living organisms," as the New Zealand government does, encompasses noise pollution handily.

The ill effects of noise pollution are documented beyond any doubt. Coming largely from transportation systems—cars and trucks mostly, but trains and buses in urban areas as well—noise pollution is proven to cause annoyance, aggression, hypertension, high stress, ringing in the ears, hearing loss, and more. One study showed that being subject to moderately high levels of noise for eight hours—as a carpenter or factory worker might be—can raise blood pressure from five to ten points and cause feelings of stress, both of which can contribute to heart disease.

Noise pollution also is thought to have serious effects on animals, which depend on hearing more acutely than humans and can find their vital hunting, self-protection, and communication abilities impaired by unnatural noise.

There is no doubt that the world is a far, far noisier place than it was before humans invented machines—especially machines with engines that propel them—and that noise has an unhealthy effect on people and animals. If loud noise doesn't seem like pollution, strictly speaking, it's probably because noise doesn't have a visible or permanent effect on our environment the way blowing trash, seeping chemicals, and oil spills do. It acts invisibly and temporarily on the air through which it moves so violently.

But that violence is felt by the ears of humans and other animals, and by our bodies in many powerful ways, most of them unhealthy. That sounds like pollution to us.

Q Is there such a thing as a blue moon?

Blue moon,
You saw me standing alone,
Without a dream in my heart,
Without a love of my own.
　　　　　—From the song "Blue Moon"

A ccording to the many performers who have recorded this Rodgers and Hart classic—including Elvis Presley, Frank Sinatra, and Bob Dylan—there most certainly is such a thing as a blue moon, and it acts as a celestial matchmaker for the lovelorn. Of course, not everyone is as sappy as the aforementioned singers. When most people mention a blue moon, they are referring to an event that is highly unusual. As our lovelorn crooners might say, "I have a date once in a blue moon."

The phrase "blue moon" dates back to 1528. It first appeared in a work by William Barlow, an English bishop, the wonderfully titled *Treatyse of the Buryall of the Masse*. "Yf they saye the mone is belewe," Barlow wrote, "we must beleve that it is true." (Trust us; he's saying something about a blue moon here.) After Barlow's usage, which no doubt confused as many readers as it edified, the term came to represent anything absurd or impossible.

It was only later that "blue moon" connoted something un-usual. Most etymologists trace this usage to the wildly popular 1819 edition of the *Maine Farmer's Almanac*, which suggested that when any season experiences four full moons (instead of the usual three), the fourth full moon was to be referred to as "blue."

As is often the case with these things, somehow the *Maine Farmer's Almanac*'s suggestion was misinterpreted—researchers blame the incompetent editors of a 1946 issue of *Sky & Telescope* magazine—to mean a second new full moon in a single month. Consequently, in present-day astronomy, that second new full moon is referred to as a "blue" moon. This frequency, ironically, isn't all that unusual, at least as astronomical events go: once every two and a half years.

As for whether the moon really can appear blue, the answer is yes. After massive forest fires swept through western Canada in 1950, for example, much of eastern North America was treated to a bluish moon in the night sky. However, events such as this occur, well, once in a blue moon.

Q What causes air turbulence?

A For even those most comfortable with flying, a sufficiently bumpy patch can lead to firmly gripped armrests and white knuckles. For anyone with a fear of flying, turbulence is the stuff of nightmares. We've been exposed to more than enough mental images, thanks to movies and television, to make it easy to envision the plane taking a sudden nosedive.

Pilots are usually quick to reassure their passengers, but they neglect to give out the information that might bring down a nervous passenger's blood pressure and put color back in his or her knuckles. Understanding turbulence might be a step toward getting over our fear of these invisible speed bumps.

Turbulence is caused by air currents moving in unpredictable ways. Airplanes achieve flight by manipulating air above and below the wings in such a way that more air flows under the wing than over, creating more air pressure under the wing than over, and thus giving the craft the ability—at the proper speed—to leave the ground. Essentially, airplanes are riding on air currents. So, when the current shifts unpredictably, the pressure around the wing changes, resulting in the turbulence you feel in the cabin.

Air currents might be moving because of a difference in temperature—warm air rises, while cool air settles. Or they might be moving over a mountain and shifting the surrounding air as they follow the jutting face of the earth. An airliner also might experience turbulence when crossing the wake of another jet or while passing currents created by violent weather patterns. If an airliner crosses a jet stream, which is a relatively narrow and fast-moving current of air caused by the earth's rotation, it will always experience turbulence (flying with a jet stream, on the other hand, is a smooth ride). Jet streams cut across the United States anywhere above twenty thousand feet, and they influence the movement of storms and other weather patterns.

Turbulence is separated into six levels of severity: Light Turbulence, Light Chop, Moderate Turbulence, Moderate Chop, Severe Turbulence, and Extreme Turbulence. The word "turbulence" here indicates a change in altitude, and as the levels get higher, the altitude changes become more pronounced. The word "chop" indicates bumpiness, without a noticeable change in altitude, similar to taking a truck through a field or down an unpaved forest trail.

In the instance of Extreme Turbulence, the aircraft is impossible to control for a period of time. The craft may suffer structural damage, and this can lead to the plane falling out of the sky. Don't lose your resolve, though—this kind of thing is rare.

If you can unclench your jaw and release your grip on the armrest, pat your frightened neighbor on the arm and explain what's happening. It might relieve his or her stress, too.

Q What would you encounter if you tried to dig a hole to China?

A Hopefully you would encounter a chiropractor, because severe back pain is about all that your journey would yield. It's obviously impossible to dig a hole to China; but for the sake of argument, we'll entertain this little gem.

Before starting, let's establish that the starting point for our hole is in the United States, where this expression appears to have originated. Nineteenth-century writer/philosopher Henry David Thoreau told the story of a crazy acquaintance who attempted to dig his way to China, and the idea apparently stuck in the American popular mind.

We also need to clear up a common misconception. On a flat map, China appears to be exactly opposite the United States. However, about five hundred years or so ago, humanity established that the earth is round, so we should know not to trust the flat representation. If you attempted to dig a hole straight down from the United States, your journey—about eight thousand miles in all—would actually end somewhere in the Indian Ocean. Therefore, our hole will run diagonally; this will have the added benefit of sparing us from having to dig through some of the really nasty parts of the earth's interior.

Anyway, let's dig. The hole starts with the crust, the outer layer of the planet that we see every day. The earth's crust is anywhere from about three to twenty-five miles thick, depending on where you are. By the time we jackhammer through this layer, the temperature will be about sixteen hundred degrees Fahrenheit—hot enough to fry us in an instant. But we digress.

The second layer of the earth is the mantle. The rock here is believed to be slightly softer than that of the crust because of the intense heat and pressure. The temperature at the mantle can exceed four thousand degrees Fahrenheit, but who's counting?

Since our hole is diagonal, we'll probably miss the earth's core. At most, we'll only have to contend with the core's outermost layer. And it's a good thing, too: Whereas the outer core is thought to be liquid, the inner core, which is about four thousand miles from the earth's surface, is believed to be made of iron and nickel, and is extremely difficult to pierce, particularly with a shovel. But either way, it would be hotter than hot; scientists think the outer core and inner core are seven thousand and nine thousand degrees Fahrenheit, respectively.

And you thought hot wings night at your local bar took a toll on your body! No, unless fire and brimstone are your thing, the only journey you'll want to take through the center of the earth is a hypothetical one.

Q Why does a red sky freak out sailors?

A We learned the rhyme in elementary school:

> Red sky at morning, sailors take warning;
> Red sky at night is a sailor's delight.

Unless your third-grade teacher was a meteorologist or a physicist, chances are you're still wondering what it means.

We'll tackle the physics first. Sunlight is made up of different colors—you've seen them all in a rainbow—and each color has its own wavelength. The blues are shorter and the reds are longer. The color that our eyes see depends on the path the light waves take and what happens to them along the way.

When the atmosphere is clean, air molecules do a good job of scattering the shorter light waves. Hence, we see a blue sky. When there's a bunch of dust and other particles—a.k.a. aerosol—in the atmosphere, those particles scatter the longer light waves; then we see a red sky.

Now we'll do the meteorology part: Our weather systems are made up of alternating high- and low-pressure areas. If you're in a high-pressure system, a low-pressure system is on either side of you, and vice versa. High-pressure areas are usually dirty—lots of aerosols—and produce clear weather. Low-pressure areas are usually clean—far fewer aerosols—and produce inclement weather.

Here's what happens when the physics and meteorology are put together: As we look at the sky at sunrise or sunset, sunlight is traveling its longest path to our eyes during the course of a day, which means it's going though more atmosphere. If we are in a mid-latitude location, say somewhere in North America or Europe, most storms travel from west to east. If the atmosphere is dirty as the light makes this long journey to our eyes, the sky will look red when the light reaches our eyes. (Remember, high-pressure area = dirty atmosphere = scattered long wavelengths = red sky.)

So, when there's a red sky to the west, there's probably a high-pressure area to the west—clear weather's ahead. But if that red sky is in the east, the high-pressure area is also in the east and a low-pressure area is on its way—a storm is coming. (And, if we're far from mid-hemisphere, exactly the opposite applies.)

By the way, rainbows can send the same weather forecast, but for different reasons. Instead of aerosols in the atmosphere and scattered light, we see rainbows because of moisture in the atmosphere and refraction—or a change in the direction—of the light. The light from the sun refracts through the moisture in the clouds in the sky opposite the sun. A rainbow in the morning when the sun is in the east can signal rain moving eastward toward you. A rainbow in the evening when the sun is in the west means that the rain has already passed you.

So a red sky or a rainbow at sunrise tells sailors who are in the mid-hemisphere in the open water looking across a long distance to the horizon that a storm is likely moving toward them. That's why sailors grow concerned and call out, "Batten down the hatches!" At sunset, that red sky or rainbow can indicate there's no storm ahead. The sailors can relax and pass the grog.

Q What's the difference between a snowstorm and a blizzard?

A If you are reading this entry, you're probably the type of person who obeys the "Ten Items or Less" signs at grocery-store checkout counters. Then again, there's something to be said for understanding exactly what words mean. So buckle up, word nerds, we're going in.

A snowstorm simply involves heavy snow. A blizzard, meanwhile, is that and more.

Some very specific conditions are required for a weather front to be called a blizzard. According to the National Weather Service (NWS), a blizzard is a snowstorm that produces large amounts of snow or blowing snow that involves winds of more than thirty-five miles per hour, reduces visibility to less than a quarter of a mile, and lasts for at least three hours. If all of these conditions are expected, the National Weather Service will issue a "Blizzard Warning." If only one or two of these conditions are expected, the NWS will toss out a piddling "Winter Storm Warning."

The word "blizzard" was first used in connection with a snowstorm (see how that works?) by an Iowa newspaper in the 1870s. Prior to this massive linguistic innovation, "blizzard" was a word used to describe a cannon or musket shot. By the 1880s, the definition of "blizzard" had stabilized into the term we all know and love.

Now that we have this one squared away, you can focus your attention on other, more important questions—such as the difference between a typhoon and a hurricane, and why you haven't had a date in twelve years.

Q Where does dew come from?

A You wake up on a cool spring morning to find the sunrise glittering over the grass, refracted in a million tiny droplets of dew. To your dismay, your father's tool set, which you neglected to put away the night before, is also glittering in the sun. It didn't rain, but everything is wet. You run out, cursing the dew for possibly ruining his best ratchet set and hoping to get the tools put away before your dad wakes up. In the midst of your cursing, you wonder: If it didn't rain, where did all the water come from?

Dew gathers primarily on cool mornings, particularly during spring and fall, when the temperature is much lower than it was the previous evening. During the heat of the day, the air is filled with water vapor. As the air cools, the land (along with the grass, trees, flowers, and your dad's tool set) cools with it.

Water vapor becomes heavier as the temperature falls. As the weight increases, the air becomes oversaturated, and when that oversaturated air comes into contact with something cool—a blade of grass, a leaf, or a socket wrench (metal loses heat quickly)—water molecules cling together and form a dew droplet. Grass and plants are usually the first to collect dew because they lose water vapor themselves, making the air above them highly saturated with water. (Oversaturated air is also what gives us clouds, mist, fog, and rain. Small droplets of condensation form mist or fog, and larger droplets form rain.)

Dew will only gather on material that has cooled, however, which is why your driveway isn't wet in the morning—a concrete slab holds heat much longer than a blade of grass. The air above the driveway is warmed by the concrete, and thus not as heavily saturated as the air over bare ground.

Which is not to say that your dad's ratchet set will be safe if you leave it on the driveway instead of the lawn. Put that thing in the shed where it belongs.

Q What is the difference between a hurricane and a typhoon?

A The short answer: There is no difference.

A hurricane is a rotating weather pattern that forms in tropical seas and can be extremely violent. The storm feeds off heat rising from the ocean and has winds of at least seventy-four miles per hour. Likewise, a typhoon is a rotating weather pattern that forms in tropical seas, can be extremely violent, and has wind gusts of at least seventy-four miles per hour. For that matter, a cyclone is a rotating weather pattern...well, you get the idea.

Here's the longer answer: The difference is in the location where the weather pattern occurs. Such a storm in the Western Hemisphere is called a hurricane; the same storm in the Eastern Hemisphere is called a typhoon (or, in some locales, a cyclone).

For the sake of argument, let's say a particularly nomadic tropical storm begins its life near the coast of Mexico. News teams might call it "Hurricane Norman." Yet if that storm packs its bags and strikes out for Japan, upon arrival it would be called "Typhoon Norman." Let's say that after a lunch of sushi and sake, "Typhoon Norman" decides it wants to experience life Down Under and headed in the direction of Australia. When it hits Sydney, newscasters would call it "Cyclone Norman." At which point, feeling a severe identity crisis coming on, "Cyclone Norman" might allow its winds to slow to a speed of less than thirty-eight miles per hour and become nothing more than a tropical depression.

The names of these storms (hurricane, typhoon, and cyclone) are also specific to language. "Hurricane" comes from the name of the Carib god of evil, *Hurican.* "Typhoon" comes from a pair of Chinese words, *taaîfung,* which translate into "great wind." "Cyclone" comes from the Greek word *kyklon,* which refers to the storm's shape rather than its winds. *Kyklon* means "circle" or "coil of a snake."

In other words, the rule when naming your tropical storms is purely geographic: location, location, location.

Chapter Eleven

MORE GOOD STUFF

Q Does a ten-gallon hat hold ten gallons?

A While we can all think of a person whose inflated ego makes him a candidate for a giant hat, let's get a little perspective: One gallon of water weighs a little more than eight pounds. Multiply that by ten, and you get just more than eighty pounds. Try to imagine anyone wearing a hat that could hold eighty pounds of water. Why, that would be like wearing...well, a ten-gallon fish tank.

What is a ten-gallon hat, anyway? It's that familiar broad-brimmed cowboy hat that we've seen in movies or on the head of the six-foot, two-inch good ol' boy who invariably sits in front of you at the game. It's said that a real cowboy might refer to his ten-gallon hat as a "John B." or a "Stetson," both of which are references to the John B. Stetson Company, the famous hatmaker. (He'll sometimes call it that even if the hat in question wasn't manufactured by Stetson.)

By now you're probably saying, "Of course. What was I thinking? It would be silly to measure a hat based on how much water it holds." Whoa, there, Mr. Haberdasher. Not so fast. One reason those particular hats originally appealed to cowboys was, in fact, their ability to hold water. The hat's high crown served as an effective bucket when thirsty horses couldn't reach water safely, or when a fire needed to be extinguished.

Duly reproached, you may now be asking, meekly, "Okay, but why ten gallons?" Nobody really knows. But fortunately for you, that doesn't stop anybody from hazarding a guess. It seems that it could be either of two cases of misunderstood Spanish. One possible explanation goes like this: Galón is a Spanish word for braid, and Mexican vaqueros (cowboys) wore as many as ten braided hatbands, or galóns, on their sombreros, depending on their proficiency in the workplace. Such a hat may have been referred to by its proud wearer as a "ten galón hat," which English-speaking cowboys then bastardized into "ten-gallon hat." (Nobody who promotes this answer ever bothers to explain why vaqueros spoke two-thirds English when discussing their hats.)

Another, perhaps slightly more plausible, guess goes like this: *Tan galan* is a Spanish phrase meaning "so gallant" that was sometimes used to describe a good-looking hat. Those same tin-eared, English-speaking cowboys heard *tan galan*, worked their magic on it, and gave us "ten gallon." (And just in case you have any shred of respect left for cowboys' Spanish-translatin' prowess: "Buckaroo" is simply an English mispronunciation of *vaquero*.)

So how much does a ten-gallon hat hold? About three quarts.

Q How do you pay through the nose?

A Very painfully. Actually, although philologists don't agree on a definitive answer, the phrase "pay through the nose," meaning to pay an exorbitant or unfair price for something, may have its origin in an excruciating procedure. According to one etymology, the unusual phrase dates back to the ninth-century occupation of Ireland by Denmark. The Danes apparently were far harsher then than they are now, and instituted something referred to as a "nose tax." Any Irishman who didn't pay this tax would be punished by having his nose slit open.

While this is an entertaining—if brutal—theory, it seems unlikely, largely because the phrase "pay through the nose" didn't appear in written English until well into the sixteen hundreds, some seven hundred years later. With this in mind, a second etymology, which is equally unprovable but much more logical, ties the phrase to the word *rhino*, which appeared in the sixteen hundreds as a slang term for money. Because *rhino* is Greek for "nose" (people used a lot more erudite slang back in the day, apparently), the terms worked themselves into a common phrase.

A third possibility suggests that "pay through the nose" is associated with the term "bleeding," as in "you're bleeding me dry." The use of bleed in reference to money first appeared in the English language at roughly the same time as "pay through the nose," and so perhaps it was the symbol of a nosebleed—both persistent and often unfair—that became associated with outrageous money expenditures.

Though the phrase "pay through the nose" may have lost its original erudite associations, the idiom is still alive and well—especially around tax time, when millions of Americans complain about the IRS "bleeding them dry." But Americans actually have it pretty good. It's not like IRS agents are ninth-century Danes or anything... even if the tax forms do seem to be written in an ancient, dead language.

Q How do dictionary writers know how to spell a word?

A How would you know if they didn't?

Dictionary writers are generally a bunch of respected scholars and smart people who are each hired to edit small sections of the dictionary (say, all the words from "ban-" to "bec-"). Not surprisingly, editing a dictionary generally requires a large amount of time devoted to reading—anything and everything. Dictionary editors might scan whatever they read for new words that are becoming popular, new uses of old words, and any spelling variants. Once that's done, the entries might be recorded in a massive database, and perhaps kept in hardcopy. This database can provide an easy reference for research about words.

A word is usually not added to the dictionary until a determination has been made that it is widely used by various sources. The choice of spelling is based on all the examples, with the most common spelling being the one used. The dictionary may also have general "house rules" about how to spell words.

Dictionary editors have some discretion in choosing spellings. An example of this is the American spelling of "color" compared to the British spelling, "colour," which goes back to Noah Webster, editor of the first American dictionary. One of Webster's pet peeves was when a word appeared to have a misleading or overly complicated spelling—too many silent letters, for example. He believed that American spelling should reflect the values of the new republic, emphasizing logical consistency and spartan simplicity. In this instance, he tried to reform the spelling by dropping the "u" from this word and others like it ("humour," for example, became "humor"). The public ran with it, and the spelling stuck. This wasn't the case, however, with some of his other reforms, such as "tung" for "tongue" and "wimmen" for "women."

Now that the printed word is ubiquitous, there are fewer spelling variations than in the distant past, when scribes would typically try to spell words according to what they heard, with no dictionaries—and certainly no Google—for checking the hard ones. Still, today's dictionary writers have their work cut out for

244 · Does Size Matter?

them. By some estimates, the English language has between 750,000 and 1,250,000 words.

Q Where can you buy truth serum?

A Contrary to what your favorite action movies and espionage novels would have you believe, truth serum is not a drug that can be purchased just about anywhere. If you suspect your spouse of being unfaithful, for example, you can't hop on down to the local grocery and pick up a bottle over the counter. Even if you somehow convince a doctor to write a prescription for the serum, you'll have difficulty procuring it. This is probably for the best, as a dose of truth serum administered by inexperienced hands could be fatal.

Truth serum, more accurately known as sodium pentothal, is a highly potent barbiturate. It got its common name (truth serum) from its use in interrogations, particularly during the Cold War. The drug impairs higher brain function. The drugged individual becomes susceptible to suggestion, possessing a weakened power of will and an extremely limited ability to refuse any manner of request. Truth serum does not force a person to tell the truth—but it does make lying difficult, and it puts the individual into a state of mind in which he or she usually is going to take the easy way out.

Created in the 1930s by scientists working for Abbott Laboratories, the drug was used initially as anesthesia. It is still used in this way, especially in cases that require fast action—such as an emergency Caesarean section—though the drug is more commonly used by veterinarians. It has also been used to induce medical comas and, in larger doses, as a lethal injection.

Sodium pentothal is no longer administered in interrogations in the United States. The Supreme Court ruled in 1963 that all confessions given under the influence of the drug are inadmissible in court. This makes sense, considering the effect of sodium pentothal is akin to a magnified state of inebriation. A suspect might be less likely to construct a cogent lie, but this does not mean that he or she is telling the truth—those who are interrogated in this manner have problems keeping fact and fantasy separated.

Abbott Laboratories continues to produce the drug, marketing it as an anesthetic and not a truth serum. To purchase it in any quantity, you must be affiliated with a hospital or the correct branch of government. Or you need to be the protagonist in an espionage novel.

Q Do straitjackets come in small, medium, and large, or are they one-size-fits-all?

A If padded decor and attendants wearing white coats are part of your everyday scene, then you're already aware that straitjackets are available in different sizes. The extra-long sleeves, which are sewn shut at each end and tied around the body, might give others the impression that your jacket comes in only one size—but you know better. You've found that in order for these sleeves to be tied securely, they must cross over your chest properly. And considering how much chest sizes vary, there are commensurate sizes, ranging from small to extra large.

The straitjacket was in vogue during the Victorian era, as a means of subduing individuals who might harm themselves or others, especially in understaffed mental institutions. Today, the strait-jacket is a favored ensemble item among professional magicians and sex fetishists, the latter preferring more titillating leather or vinyl styles. As a result, there are a number of straitjacket vendors from which to choose. On one Web site, a small straitjacket is for those with a chest of thirty-two to thirty-eight inches; medium is thirty-seven to forty-four; large is forty-three to forty-eight; and extra large is forty-seven to fifty-two.

Whatever the motivation—crazy or kinky—confinement is the name of the straitjacket game. To create a binding effect, the jacket, especially the chest and armholes, must fit tightly; this makes it more difficult for the wearer to pull his or her arms free. The person's arms are folded across the front of the body, and the sleeve ends are wrapped around to fasten behind the back. Some versions feature sleeves that are threaded through front and/or side loops to prevent the arms from being raised overhead. Other common restraint features include thick canvas material for sturdy wear, back straps, friction buckles, and a crotch strap.

For illusionists who specialize in escapes, there is no substitute for an authentic J. T. Posey straitjacket. This version produces the truest institutional silhouette and is considered the most difficult from which to break free. It features four back straps, an arm loop, and arm straps. Posey sizes tend to run a bit small, which could be of slight concern since a jacket shrinks about 10 percent after washing. A Posey will set you back $200 to $250.

It's a tough time to be in the straitjacket business. As iconic as it is, the straitjacket is receding into history. Just as fur products have met opposition from animal rights groups in recent decades, the straitjacket has come under fire as well. Organizations such as the National Alliance on Mental Illness want to put the archaically negative images of straitjackets to rest and promote modern drug and rehabilitative therapies, which have connotations that are much more positive.

So if you're still lumbering around in that tired old straitjacket, consider shedding it—with a little assistance, of course—and trying a new approach. Mental makeovers are all the rage, baby.

Q How many kids have had an eye put out by a BB gun?

A In any BB gun discussion, anywhere in the Western world (presumably), it's only a matter of time before someone quotes *A Christmas Story*. Ralphie, the movie's main character, wants nothing on earth so much as a BB gun. But every time he voices his desire, his mother has five words for him: "You'll shoot your eye out!" The line has become a mantra for concerned mothers—a classic BB gun block. When it comes to real kids in real backyards shooting real BB guns, how plausible is this concern?

Unfortunately for every ten-year-old who has ever petitioned his parents for one of these toy rifles, his mother's concern is somewhat justified. According to a report filed by the Centers for Disease Control and Prevention, there were more than forty-seven thousand BB gun–related injuries to children and teenagers treated in emergency rooms across the country between June 1992 and May 1994. Of these, 2,839 (about 6 percent) involved an injury to the eye. It's a rather small figure compared to injuries sustained to the arms, legs, hands, and feet, however; shots to the extremities comprised 54 percent of the reported injuries.

As famous as the mantra has become, shots to the eye are not the only ones to cause serious harm. There have been cases of BBs penetrating deep enough to become lodged in vital organs, and a report issued in 2004 quotes an average of four deaths a year due to BB guns and other nonpowder rifles (those that fire by use of a spring, pressurized CO_2, or pressurized air).

BB guns can be harmless toys when used properly, under the supervision of a mature adult, but their dangerous aspects should not be downplayed. Use of safety glasses and thick, protective clothing can reduce the risk of injury, but teaching safe conduct and respect for guns (even when they only fire BBs) is the best way to avoid a trip to the local emergency room.

More than three million nonpowder rifles are sold every year. Many are sold in department stores and toy stores, and many are sold to kids. Most states have no age restrictions when it comes to the sale of BB guns. If these kids are not taught how to respect their guns, it may not be long before the toys are banned altogether. In fact, the state of New York has already done so.

"You'll shoot your eye out!" may be the easiest way to shoot down a ten-year-old's dream of owning a BB gun, but it's one of the least likely outcomes. Not every child with a BB gun is going to injure himself. And, in the event of an injury, it's much more likely that the BB will end up lodged in an extremity. Maybe the mantra should be changed to, "You'll shoot your palm and end up with a metal ball trapped just below the skin for the rest of your life."

On second thought, we like the other mantra better.

Q If nobody buys a ticket, do they still show the movie?

A This question is so easy to answer, it really shouldn't be asked. Or should it? The answer is "yes" or "um, maybe," depending on whether the movie theater is corporately owned or an independent. According to the delightful and well-informed customer service reps at Regal Entertainment Group, owner and operator of the largest theater circuit in the United States, the show must go on!

Movie presentations in all 527 Regal theaters are pre-set. It's the twenty-first century, remember—hardly any manual labor is required because the projectors are all computerized. So it doesn't matter if fifty patrons purchase tickets to see a movie on any of Regal's 6,388 screens, if one couple purchases tickets, or no one purchases a ticket—the entire presentation, including the commercials and previews, will run its pre-set course.

Now for the "maybe." There are thousands of independent movie theaters in the United States—the exact figure is unknown. Some are small and seedy, and may seat no more than fifty; others are more spacious and pristine, and seat several hundred. In these movie houses, decisions about whether to show a movie if no one buys a ticket are at the discretion of the theater's management.

Q If the cops break down your door, do they have to pay for it?

A It's not unprecedented. But don't expect any of those polite officers to take time out to write you a check while they're barreling through your house. You're going to need to hire a lawyer.

Generally speaking, in cases that involve the police causing damage to private property, they're covered by a couple of legal precepts known as governmental tort immunity and sovereign immunity. Tort immunity exempts the government from having to pay for damages (it also allows the government to get away with a bunch of other stuff, but that's another story). Sovereign immunity lets the government decide whether you can sue the government. You can probably guess what the government usually decides.

Let's say you are allowed to sue. You need to prove that the cops were being negligent when they broke down your door. And history has shown (to the relief of taxpayers everywhere) that in cases of simple property damage, it's fairly rare for a court to find that police were negligent. Even if the cops break down your door and then realize they've made a mistake and really meant to break down your neighbor's door, that's still considered to be a reasonable execution of their duties.

What constitutes negligence? One example would be an officer who breaks down your door without a warrant and without a pressing need to get in immediately. If you're "lucky" enough to have that happen, well, you may be the winner of a government-subsidized shopping spree in the door department at Home Depot.

In recent years, some state and local governments have moved to scale back governmental tort immunity. But even in those places, the people who benefit from government settlements tend to be the people who suffered most—those who were injured or had relatives who were killed or were subject to extreme violations of their civil rights. When it comes to busted doors, the government still probably won't show you a whole lot of sympathy.

Q Who gets the royalties when "God Bless America" is sung?

A The Boys Scouts of America and the Girl Scouts of America are the lucky recipients. But why?

In 1938, singer Kate Smith asked composer Irving Berlin to write her a patriotic song to sing on Armistice Day (which is what Veterans' Day was called before World War II). Berlin agreed,

though not because he needed the job. He was wildly successful—huge hits on Broadway and in the movies had made him
the most famous songwriter in America, and he was married to
a wealthy heiress to boot. He still loved his work, however, and
patriotism was his middle name.

Berlin remembered a song he had composed and filed away
many years before. It was written for the finale of a World War
I musical called *Yip, Yip, Yaphank*, but it seemed a little over the
top in 1918. He polished up that song, "God Bless America," and
presented it to Kate Smith. She was delighted and sang it on her
radio show—not just on Armistice Day but every week. The song
was a smash.

But who would get the royalties? Berlin decided immediately
that they should go to charity. The idea of using the proceeds
to benefit the youth of America appealed to him, so he set up a
trust fund and put journalist Herbert Bayard Swope in charge,
along with Colonel Theodore Roosevelt (son of the first President
Roosevelt) and boxer Gene Tunney—a group chosen to represent
Jewish, Catholic, and Protestant denominations. They came up
with the idea to give all the royalties to the Boy Scouts and Girls
Scouts.

To this day, the God Bless America Fund owns the copyright to
the song. Before September 11, 2001, "God Bless America"
had raised more than six million dollars for the scout groups.
After that tragedy, the song surged in popularity once more, as
recordings by Céline Dion, LeAnn Rimes, and other stars moved
listeners and shot up the charts. With the royalties still pouring
in, scouting will no doubt thrive throughout the twenty-first
century.

Q Why are coffins six feet under?

A We've all heard the line in a cheesy movie that, against our better judgment, has sucked us in and stuck us to the couch: "One more move, and I'll put you six feet under." Whether the words are growled by a cowboy in a black hat or a mobster in pinstripes, everyone knows what those six feet represent: the depth where coffins reside after burial.

Or do they?

The bad guy may well mean what he says, but the final resting place for someone unfortunate enough to be in a coffin varies depending on the site of the funeral. Burial depths can range from eighteen inches to twelve feet. There's no world council that has decreed that a person must be put to rest exactly six feet under. Think about it. Digging a six-foot grave in a region below sea level, such as New Orleans, would get pretty soggy. (Of course, a corpse floating up from the grave might add some flair to that cheesy movie.)

Most grave depths are determined by local, state, or national governments. New Orleans has dealt with its topographical issues by placing most of its dead above ground in crypts. The area's gravesites in the ground are almost always less than two feet deep—and even that doesn't prevent the occasional floater.

The California requirement is a mere eighteen inches. In Quebec, Canada, the law states that coffins "shall be deposited in a grave and covered with at least one meter of earth" (a little more than three feet). This is similar to New South Wales in Australia, which calls for nine hundred millimeters (slightly less than three feet). And the Institute of Cemetery and Crematorium Management in London says that "no body shall be buried in such a manner that any part of the coffin is less than three feet below the level of any ground adjoining the grave."

If burial depths vary from place to place, how did the phrase "six feet under" come to life? (Sorry, couldn't resist.) Historians believe it originated in England. London's Great Plague of 1665 killed seventy-five thousand to one hundred thousand people. In Daniel Defoe's book *A Journal of the Plague Year*, he writes that the city's lord mayor issued an edict that all graves had to be dug six feet deep to limit the spread of the plague outbreak. Other sources confirm Defoe's claim.

Of course, the plague is a scourge of the past, and today's world has no uniform burial depth. But who really cares? It still makes for a winning line in an otherwise schlocky movie.

Q Why don't school buses have seatbelts?

A No, it is not for freedom of movement while aiming a spitball. Buses are actually quite safe, thanks to a design that helps make up for the lack of seatbelts. Adding seatbelts wouldn't make them much safer, as it turns out, and would actually introduce some tricky challenges.

School buses are the safest way for a child to get to school—safer than walking, riding a bike, and, yup, being driven by a parent. More than forty-two thousand people die in motor-vehicle accidents every year, according to the National Highway Traffic Safety Administration (NHTSA), but on average only six children die in school-bus accidents. Teens who drive themselves to school are one hundred times more likely to be killed than if they rode the bus. Why are children safer on the bus? Buses are bigger and higher than most other cars on the road, and they move at slower speeds. School busses also employ a safety feature called "compartmentalization."

Compartmentalization describes the little nooks and crannies that bus seats create. The seats are firmly anchored, have high backs, are filled with impact-absorbent material, and are spaced closely together. This creates individual spaces that, for the most part, keep children from being thrown forward; the kids just ricochet between the two seats. The study that suggested this form of compartmentalization was conducted in 1967 by UCLA engineers. The researchers advised using seat backs eight inches higher than what buses ended up with. They also suggested a side-padded bar to help with side collisions and rollovers, as well as a lap belt. So, the current design isn't as safe as it could be.

The NHTSA did a study that found seatbelts would reduce the annual number of fatalities by one. But lap belts alone would cause more injuries to the neck and head if they were not worn properly, which brings up another issue: Who's going to make sure the seatbelts are adjusted and worn correctly? A single bus driver can't make sure that fifty students are wearing their belts correctly. It isn't an efficient use of time, and those drivers put up with enough already. Seatbelts add thousands of dollars to the cost of a bus (just ask California, New York, New Jersey, and Florida, the four states that have laws requiring belts on new buses).

The most dangerous part of riding the bus is getting on and off. According to the NHTSA, four times more kids are killed outside the bus than inside—by either the bus itself or a car that didn't stop for the bus. Seatbelts wouldn't reduce this number.

Seatbelts also wouldn't reduce instances of sitting in gum, getting your hair pulled, or being called names. They could, however, reduce the incidents of one kid giving another a wedgie, so maybe they are worth additional consideration.

Q Why do people yell "Geronimo!" when they jump from a high place?

A Geronimo was a Native American military leader and medicine man of the Bedonkohe Apaches who defended his people's land against invading settlers. Born in June 1829 as Goyathlay, he got the name "Geronimo" after a particularly brutal 1851 battle with Mexicans who attacked his camp and killed his wife and kids. Geronimo continued to fight the attackers with a knife during a hail of gunfire, ignoring their cries of "Geronimo"—which were probably appeals to Saint Jerome. The name stayed with him for the rest of his life.

But what does a Native American leader have to do with jumping? The connection began when Paramount Studios released a Western in 1939 titled *Geronimo*. At the time, the U.S. Army had just formed its first paratrooper platoon. The test unit trained at Fort Benning, Georgia. To relieve tension after a long, hot day, the paratroopers often spent their evenings in the local movie theater.

In August 1940, four paratroopers saw the movie *Geronimo*. During their walk back to the base, someone asked Private Aubrey Eberhardt if he was scared about their first mass jump the next day. Private Eberhardt insisted that he wasn't. Inspired by the film, he said that he would yell out "Geronimo!" right after he jumped to prove that he had kept himself together. The next day, the others heard him yelling during the jump, and the practice spread among other paratroopers.

By 1941, the name "Geronimo" was part of the insignia of the 501st Parachute Infantry Battalion, and was eventually incorporated into other units' mottos and insignias. A song about the 11th Airborne Division called "Down from Heaven" included these lyrics: "Down from heaven comes eleven/and there's hell to pay below/shout 'Geronimo' 'Geronimo.'"

Those early paratroopers got so much media attention during the war that civilians picked up the cry. Today, it can be heard at just about any public pool as kids launch themselves off diving boards. Perhaps these young daredevils would be better off yelling something that derives from the word Saint Michael rather than Saint Jerome. Saint Michael, after all, is the patron saint of paratroopers—and other airborne people.

Q Why does an orchestra conductor need a baton?

A So there was this seventeenth-century composer named Jean-Baptiste Lully who was conducting his beautiful music at a rehearsal. As always, he was keeping time with a huge wooden staff that he pounded on the floor. On this fateful day, however, Lully missed the floor and drove the staff right into his foot.

No, this is not the moment the conductor's baton was born. Lully did not have an epiphany and say, "You know, I should use something smaller to direct my music."

Nevertheless, the moment remains part of music history. An abscess developed on Lully's right foot that turned to gangrene. The composer did not have the foot amputated, causing the gangrene to spread and eventually leading to his death. There you have it—a conducting fatality!

So when did conductors trade in those clumsy, and potentially lethal, wooden staffs for the symbolically powerful batons? And do they really need them? Don't a conductor's hands contain ten God-made batons?

Some conductors today use their hands and fingers, but most have a baton that they move to the music. The feeling is that the baton—usually ten to twenty-four inches long and made of wood, fiberglass, or carbon—magnifies a conductor's patterns and gestures, making them clearer for the orchestra or ensemble.

Orchestras date to the late sixteenth century during the Baroque period, and conductors back then used the same type of staff that felled Lully. Sometimes there was no conductor at all. Instead, the leader was most often a keyboardist, who would guide the orchestra when his hands were free, or a violinist, who would set the tempo and give directions by beating the neck of his instrument or making other movements. At other times, the keyboardist or violinist simply played louder so the rest of the orchestra could follow his lead.

As written music grew more complex, orchestras needed more direction than a keyboardist or violinist could provide. Conductors started appearing in France in the eighteenth century and emerged in earnest early in the nineteenth century. Still, there was no baton—rolled up paper was the tool of choice.

German composer, violinist, and conductor Louis Spohr claimed to have introduced the formal baton to the music world in a performance in 1820, but that simply might have been boastfulness. It is widely thought that he only used a baton in rehearsals.

It's possible that German composer, pianist, and conductor Felix Mendelssohn was the first to use an actual baton in a performance. According to *The Cambridge Companion to Conducting*, Mendelssohn used a baton in 1829 and again in 1832 with the Philharmonic Society of London. The next year, a baton was used regularly with the Philharmonic—and today, almost every conductor wields one.

Even though the baton is a lot safer than the wooden staff, there have been some accidents along the way. For example, German conductor Daniel Turk's motions became so animated during a performance in 1810 that he hit a chandelier above his head and was showered with glass. What is it with these guys?

There was more baton craziness in 2006 and 2007. First, the conductor of the Harvard University band set a record by using a baton that was ten and one-half or twelve and one-half feet long, depending on whom you listen to. The next year, the University of Pennsylvania band claimed to have bested that record with its fifteen-foot, nine-inch baton. There were no reports of a Lully moment on either occasion.

Q Why is it always a band's drummer who kicks the bucket?

A In order to answer this question, we need to first answer why it's being asked in the first place. There are several good reasons.

First of all, when it comes to rock bands—no, when it comes to seminal British hard-rock bands—it does seem like the drummer's always kicking the bucket in grand fashion. The Who's gifted drummer, Keith Moon, died in 1978, just weeks after the release of *Who Are You*, of an overdose of pills he was taking to combat alcoholism. There's a grim irony right there.

In 1980, Led Zeppelin's brilliant beat-keeper, John "Bonzo" Bonham, went to his eternal reward after a day of prodigious drinking. He began the morning with four quadruple vodkas and a ham roll. "Breakfast," he said to his assistant, after a bite of the ham roll. He drank throughout the day and night and was found dead the next morning, having choked on his own vomit.

These legendary codas, if you will, were surely on the mind of Rob Reiner and his writing partners when they scripted the 1984 "rockumentary" *This Is Spinal Tap*. As of the filming, Spinal Tap had lost three drummers: John "Stumpy" Pepys (in a bizarre gardening accident); Eric "Stumpy Joe" Childs (who

choked on someone else's vomit); and Peter "James" Bond (who spontaneously combusted onstage). If the actual deaths of Moon and Bonham didn't confirm the impression that rock drummers meet untimely ends, then *Spinal Tap* did.

But there are other likely contributing factors. One is that drummers are widely perceived as being slightly "off." More jokes are told at drummers' expense than anyone else's. Two examples:

- How can you tell whether the stage is level? The drummer is drooling out of both sides of his mouth.
- What do you call a drummer who just broke up with his girlfriend? Homeless.

You get the idea.

Other explanations are plausible. A neurologist might suggest that the constant pounding a drummer creates and endures behind the skins rattles his brain, so to speak. (No self-respecting neurologist would use that term unless he was himself drunk—or drumming.)

A neuropsychologist might suggest that drummers often suffer from sensory-integration issues, and that while drumming would be a form of self-therapy, the wider sensory-integration problems might contribute to some sort of instability in those drummers. Or the neuropsychologist might keep quiet.

In fact, a wider look at the phenomenon of dramatic premature deaths in rock and roll suggests that drummers are no more likely to die than any other band member. AC/DC's dynamic frontman, Bon Scott, died a few months before Zeppelin's Bonham, of acute alcohol poisoning. Ten years before Scott passed into the next world, guitar genius Jimi Hendrix died in circumstances shrouded in some mystery, but by various accounts involving wine, sleeping pills, and tuna sandwiches. In 1974, singer "Mama" Cass Elliot died of a heart attack in the same hotel room Moon would die in four years later.

Drummers none of them.

So while there are many compelling reasons why there's a perception that it's always a band's drummer who kicks the bucket, the reality is something different. Kicking the bucket seems to happen to all sorts of folks in rock; it's almost as common as sex and drugs.

Q Are tumbleweeds alive?

A Yes, indeed. But probably not when you're likely to notice them—rolling and bouncing in the breeze across a highway somewhere in the rural United States. The skinny, spiky ball of twigs stuck under the front fender of your car is dead. That tumbleweed, however, had an interesting life. It was quite pretty when in bloom, and there's a chance that it helped the planet remain a little safer from long-term radiation.

And here you thought a tumbleweed's only use was to provide the proper Old West aura for John Wayne movies, right? With apologies to the Duke, the tumbleweed deserves a better introduction. The first thing you should know is that the tumbleweed—actually called Russian thistle—originally was an alien that wound up in America by accident and made its way to dry, salient land because it is remarkably salt-tolerant.

Oh, and it's correct to call it a weed. In fact, when the species *salsola tragus* turned up in 1877 as a stowaway, along with some flaxseed imported by Ukrainian farmers, around Bon Homme County, South Dakota, the newcomer was super-invasive. Several types of the plant became so abundant in various parts of North America that the U.S. Department of Agriculture eventually listed it as a "noxious weed" in the most afflicted areas.

Russian thistle grows to about three feet high and can reach five feet, blooms in spring, and then breaks off at the base when the plant has matured in late summer. The shrubs can be particularly annoying in autumn, when it's almost impossible to drive on some roads without steering through a barrage of tumbleweeds. Most people consider the weeds simply a nuisance—though the city of Chandler, Arizona, constructs its official Christmas tree from tumbleweeds each year.

Another use for this humble plant goes far beyond amusing the residents of Chandler. For reasons no one can explain, Russian thistle soaks up depleted uranium from contaminated soil—making it useful for reducing long-term toxicity at weapons-testing grounds and battlefields.

Depleted uranium is used in armor-piercing munitions, and though it produces only low levels of radiation, it can pose a hazard by seeping into the soil. "There is some use to what we consider noxious weeds," geologist Dana Ulmer-Scholle of the New Mexico Institute of Mining and Technology declared in

Science Daily. The U.S. Department of Defense funded a 2004 study in which Ulmer-Scholle and several colleagues proved that Russian thistle sucked up depleted uranium—and that sprinkling the ground with citric acid enhanced the plant's ability to absorb the uranium.

Come to think of it, maybe John Wayne would be proud of the patriotic tumbleweed. Remember that when three or four of the things come hopping across your windshield.

Q What happens to those socks that get lost in the dryer?

A Dogs eat them. Aliens abduct them. The heat and rapid spinning motions of the dryer transport them to an alternate space-time continuum. Or maybe they wind up in the Bermuda Triangle or on a giant sock dune on the planet Saturn.

Of course, there's always the option they've simply departed this physical world for that great big sock drawer in the sky. May 9 is officially Lost Sock Memorial Day. Come to think of it, one of those TV news magazine shows should really investigate the possibility of a sock suicide pact. Hey, if you spent your days warming the sweaty toes of some smelly teenager, wouldn't you consider checking out early?

Short of sending Geraldo Rivera undercover as a 100 percent stretch nylon Gold Toe (we could spin him around in a Maytag to see what happens), is there any way to know where all the lost socks go? There's got to be a logical explanation, right?

Well, conspiracy theorists maintain it all has to do with a long-time clandestine concordat between America's sock weavers and the major appliance makers. Have they created some sort of top-secret sock material and patented tumbling action that makes our anklets, crews, and knee-highs disintegrate into thin air?

Strange how socks seem to go missing without leaving a single thread of evidence behind. You can sweep that laundry room with the precision of a forensic scientist at a crime scene. The only clue you'll uncover in this case: U.S. sock sales amount to about $4.9 billion annually. Hmm...

Of course, reps from both sides adamantly deny any wrongdoing in the disappearance of perhaps millions of American socks over the years. In fact, executives at Michigan-based Whirlpool say, it's not them, "it's you." According to Whirlpool, most often your dirty socks don't even make it to the machine. They fall out of the laundry basket in a trail behind you on the way to the washer. Or your kids shoot them around like basketballs so they end up under the bed. Research by Whirlpool's Institute of Fabric Science also reveals static cling is a culprit. When socks pairs do make it to the dryer, static can send one up a pant leg and the other into the corner pocket of a fitted sheet.

What's the solution? Whirlpool recommends placing socks in mesh laundry bags, while Linda Cobb, a DIY Network host and the author of *Talking Dirty Laundry with the Queen of Clean*, advocates the use of sock clips. These are designed to keep single pairs of socks together as they wash and dry.

Of course, clipping each and every pair of socks in the family hamper is going to be time-consuming—and who knows if it'll even work? It would be a whole lot easier to just accept that all those lost socks were taken by the "little people." You do know that gnomes, leprechauns, and pixies turn stolen socks into cozy blankets for their wee offspring, right?

Q Why is it good to be a wise man but not a wise guy?

A To be sure, there's a stark contrast here—the former is a smart person, the latter is a smart aleck. The sayings of a wise man should be ignored at one's own peril, while the sayings of a wise guy should be ignored, period. But taken at face value, shouldn't the two refer to the same thing (that thing, of course, being a person of great wisdom)? Well, that's the funny thing about colloquial English: Appearances are often deceiving.

When reference is made to a wise man, it's safe to say everyone within hearing distance is on the same page. A wise man is one who is savvy to the ways of the world. This dates back to Biblical times, when three wise men (also referred to as the Magi) followed a star to the birthplace of Jesus. They were called "wise men" because they practiced astrology and divination and were rumored to have supernatural knowledge. (The origin of the word "Magi"—*Magus*—is the same as the origin of the word "magician.")

The wise guy, as we have come to know him, is a much younger specimen. His origins are harder to pin down. The term "wise guy," meant ironically, was part of the American vernacular by the end of the nineteenth century. It is most likely a derivation of the term "wiseacre," which has the same meaning: Both refer to one who puts up a pretense of knowledge, especially in a specific area, to mask one's own ignorance. Wiseacre most likely comes from the Middle Dutch word *wijssegger*—pronounced *wai-zegger*. *Wijssegger* refers to a soothsayer or a prophet; in English, it has always been used ironically. This twisted translation appeared in English for the first time in 1595, in a popular ballad.

The reason for this ironic translation is most likely due to age-old enmity between the English and the Dutch. There are many phrases in the English language in which Dutch people are referred to in a derogatory manner: "Dutch courage" is the courage one acquires through alcohol consumption; a "Dutch nightingale" is a frog; and a "Dutch concert" is a particularly offensive cacophony. Quoting the Dutch word for wise man, but meaning the opposite, is probably nothing more than a jab at Dutch intelligence.

Though the origins are murky, the difference is clear: Heed the message of the wise man; disregard that of the wise guy. And take what the English say about the Dutch with a grain of salt.

CONTRIBUTORS

Angelique Anacleto specializes in style and beauty writing. She has written for leading salon industry publications and is currently working on a children's book.

Brett Ballantini is a sportswriter who has written for several major sports teams and has authored a book titled *The Wit and Wisdom of Ozzie Guillen.*

Diane Lanzillotta Bobis is a food, fashion, and lifestyle writer from Glenview, Illinois.

Joshua D. Boeringa is a writer living in Mt. Pleasant, Michigan. He has written for magazines and Web sites.

Michelle Burton is a writer and editor with one foot in Chicago and the other in Newport Beach, California. She has written guidebooks and hundreds of feature articles and reviews.

Steve Cameron is a writer living in Cullen, Scotland. He has written thirteen books, and is a former columnist and reporter for several American newspapers and magazines.

Anthony G. Craine is a contributor to the *Britannica Book of the Year* and has written for magazines including *Inside Sports* and *Ask.* He is a former United Press International bureau chief.

Dan Dalton is a writer and editor living in the Pacific Northwest.

Shanna Freeman is a writer and editor living near Atlanta. She also works in an academic library.

Chuck Giametta is a highly acclaimed journalist who specializes in coverage of the automotive industry. He has written and edited books, magazines, and Web articles on many automotive topics.

Ed Grabianowski writes about science and nature, history, the automotive industry, and science fiction for Web sites and magazines. He lives in Buffalo, New York.

Jack Greer is a writer living in Chicago.

Tom Harris is a Web project consultant, editor, and writer living in Atlanta. He is the co-founder of Explainst.com, and was head of the editorial content team at HowStuffWorks.com.

Vickey Kalambakal is a writer and historian based in Southern California. She writes for textbooks, encyclopedias, magazines, and ezines.

Brett Kyle is a writer living in Draycott, Somerset, England. He also is an actor, musician, singer, and playwright.

Noah Liberman is a Chicago-based sports, entertainment, and business writer who has published two books and has contributed articles to a wide range of newspapers and national magazines.

Letty Livingston is a dating coach, relationship counselor, and sexpert. Her advice column, Let Letty Help, has been published in more than forty periodicals and on the Internet (letlettyhelp.blogspot.com).

Jeff Moores is an illustrator whose work appears in periodicals and advertisements, and as licensed characters on clothing. Visit his Web site (jeffmoores.com) to see more of his work.

Alex Nechas is a writer and editor based in Chicago.

Jessica Royer Ocken is a freelance writer and editor based in Chicago.

Thad Plumley is an award-winning writer who lives in Dublin, Ohio. He is the director of publications and information products for the National Ground Water Association.

ArLynn Leiber Presser is a writer living in suburban Chicago. She is the author of twenty-seven books.

Pat Sherman is a writer living in Cambridge, Massachusetts. She is the author of several books for children, including *The Sun's Daughter* (Clarion, 2005) and *Ben and the Proclamation of Emancipation* (Eerdmans, 2009).

Carrie Williford is a writer living in Atlanta. She was a contributing writer to HowStuffWorks.com.

Factual verification: Darcy Chadwick, Barbara Cross, Bonny M. Davidson, Brenda McLean, Carl Miller, Katrina O'Brien, Marilyn Perlberg